12-17

To Thomas Rooney –

Much appreciation for your dedication to New York's first responders.

Your commitment is what keeps the memory of our loved ones alive.

With heartfelt thanks,
Kathleen

Life Detonated

The True Story of a Widow and a Hijacker

Kathleen Murray Moran

Amberjack Publishing
New York, New York

Amberjack Publishing
228 Park Avenue S #89611
New York, NY 10003-1502
http://amberjackpublishing.com

This is a work of creative nonfiction. It is nonfiction in that this is a true story based on the author's memories, and creative in that the author has expanded on her memory to build a richer narrative. The events contained herein are accurate to the best of the author's memory. Minor details which do not impact the story have been changed as necessary to protect the privacy of those involved.

Publisher's Cataloging-in-Publication data

Names: Moran, Kathleen Murray, author.
Title: Life detonated : the true story of a widow and a hijacker / by Kathleen Murray Moran.
Description: New York, NY: Amberjack Publishing, 2017.
Identifiers: ISBN 978-1-944995-32-4 (Hardcover) | 978-1-944995-45-4 (pbk.) | 978-1-944995-36-2 (ebook) | LCCN 2017934572
Subjects: LCSH Moran, Kathleen Murray. | Police spouses--Family relationships--United States. | Police--Family relationships--United States. | Terrorism--New York (State)--New York--History. | Police--New York (State)--New York--History. | Bombings--United States--Personal Narratives. | Hijacking of aircraft--United States--Personal narratives. | Police--Violence against--New York (State)--New York. | BISAC BIOGRAPHY & AUTOBIOGRAPHY / Personal Memoirs | BIOGRAPHY & AUTOBIOGRAPHY / Law Enforcement
Classification: LCC HV7921 .M672 2017 | DDC 301.42--dc23

Cover Design: Black Kat Creative
*Jacket Image: Deconstructed Sphere, 2005 (acrylic) by Lincoln Seligman /
Bridgeman Images*

To my husband, James, my children, Keith, Christopher, and Kaitlin, and my grandchildren, Olivia, Finnegan, and Lillian.

Author's Note

Life Detonated is a true story of the events of September 11, 1976. Some information has been reprinted from newspapers. The hijacker, Julie Busic, has consented to the use of her letters.

The names of my siblings have been changed to protect their anonymity, but all other names are accurate.

Writing a memoir requires re-imagination. It is not possible to perceive reality directly without filtering or embellishment, without which this book would be flat and uninteresting.

I don't remember everything about my past. No one does. But I do remember the run in my mother's nylon stockings as she walked out of the kitchen without addressing the cast on my broken arm. I remember watching her smoke a cigarette on my back porch, shivering as she smashed the red tip into the wooden railing, knowing she longed for a place of her own.

All of what I write in this book is the truth as I remember it. That doesn't mean someone else will read the same passage and say it didn't happen that way. That's the beauty of memoir. It is truth reimagined. The stories are as I reimagine them. I never cross the line and make up stories, but I do embellish details, and added dialogue that obviously could not have been word-for-word, but is close enough.

Most of what I write about the hijacker has been taken from her letters and some information from her book. All of it is true, but it is the truth as I know it.

The stories about my family tell an emotional truth, how I felt, and what I remember happening right in front of me. But these memories, too, can be tricky, if only because they happened a half century ago. I could not have gotten it all straight, so I went for the impact of how it felt.

Mimi Schwartz, who writes on memoir, said, "The subconscious is remembering." And that's where the memories were stored before I tried to bring them to the page. Subconscious was all I had to rely on, and I wrote my story to the best of my re-imagination.

Prologue

THEY SAY THE GRIEF THAT COMES WITH DEATH DOUBLES back on you and makes you mourn again all those past disappointments and tiny deaths you never had the chance to fully reconcile. But what I've come to wonder is if death might be a birthing room, or a gift. It is a sad and heartbreaking gift, and yet the aftermath of death allows us to understand the tenacity and fortitude of the human spirit. It may be true to say we are presented again and again with small deaths—hijackings perhaps—chances to either lie down and surrender, or be reborn again. And to lift ourselves out of those frequent small deaths, or out of something as horrifying as a bomb exploding in the middle of the night, or a terrorist attack on a passenger plane, we must come to understand that we really do have the strength to make the choice to live again.

Do not go gentle into that good night.
Rage, rage against the dying of the light.
— Dylan Thomas, *Do Not Go*
Gentle Into That Good Night

We Lost Him

September 11, 1976

I was lying perfectly still in a lavender-scented bath thinking about the man who would slip into bed with me in another hour, run his hand down my back until I turned around, show me that sheepish grin, and kiss me with those lips that tasted like Lucky Strikes and smelled like the night air. I traced the constellation of freckles along my chest that he would outline with his fingers after we made love. We were trying for a girl. We had been hoping for a girl since our second son was born two years before.

"This is a special report from CBS News. TWA flight 355 to Chicago carrying eighty-six passengers and seven crew members has been hijacked." I opened my eyes to hear the eleven o'clock news coming from our bedroom. "Shortly after takeoff from New York's LaGuardia Airport at 8:00 p.m., the aircraft was commandeered by Zvonko and Julie Busic, a Croatian and his American wife. They claim to have a bomb on board the plane and a second device located in New York City." I stood up, grabbed a towel, and ran into the bedroom.

The camera left Walter Cronkite and panned Grand Central

1

Station, and the most familiar face in the world to me came into focus: my husband Brian in a Kevlar vest, "Bomb Squad" written on the back. Bath water dripped onto the rug as I stared at the tiny black-and-white TV. The scene panned across a row of twenty-five cent luggage lockers, the doors torn off their hinges, to Brian lifting a shopping bag from inside one of the lockers. The white Macy's bag looked harmless. NYPD uniforms crowded around as Brian placed the bag on top of the bomb blanket and clipped the ends together. I watched as he and Hank Dworkin threaded a long pole into the blanket's loops and balanced it across their shoulders. The camera followed them to the disposal truck parked outside Grand Central where they disappeared from my view.

Backing away from the TV, I sat on the bed holding the towel in a tight ball. *Croatia? Where was it—Yugoslavia? Stay calm*, I told myself. Brian worked hundreds of bomb cases. All of them were dangerous. He always assured me he never took risks. *Don't panic.* I had dipped chicken in breadcrumbs that afternoon and made potato salad for our picnic at the beach tomorrow. *Wait for him to call.* But, without knowing why, this time felt different.

Down the hall, in the glow of the tiny nightlight, our four-year-old son Keith slept, his sheets tangled around his legs, his forehead damp from the heat that our ceiling fan did little to ease. It was so hot the blacktop stuck to his sneakers, Brian told me that afternoon before he left for work. Chris, the baby, was snuggled at the top of his crib, his hands under his chin as though in prayer. I stood in the doorway watching them sleep, and listening to them breathe.

Back in the bedroom I dropped the towel and pulled a nightgown from the dresser drawer. The hijacking was still unfolding on the TV. It was almost midnight. The news should have been over. Brian should have been on his way home. I crawled into bed, shivering despite the day's heat, and reminded myself the bomb squad had lost two men in its entire history, and that was back in '39 at the World's Fair.

Still, there was LaGuardia last December, when a bomb detonated in a luggage locker. Twenty-five sticks of dynamite shattered the TWA terminal, killing eleven people, injuring hundreds. A makeshift morgue was set up in the airport, and Brian waited all night as the medical examiner extracted pieces of the bomb from the dead. The case remained unsolved. TWA. LaGuardia. Coincidence?

I looked over at the dress shirts in Brian's closet, lined up like mock military soldiers, his wing tips polished, waiting for their rotation. "Come home," I whispered into the dark. When I closed my eyes, I saw that Macy's shopping bag with its cheerful red star.

I woke to red lights flashing off our bedroom walls. I could almost feel them crawling across my face. I thought I heard the swishing of clothes, the soft drop of rubber-soled shoes. The clock said 4:00 a.m.

When I pulled back the curtains, I saw police cars scattered along the street below, doors left ajar. Red lights moved in unrelenting slow circles. The doorbell echoed up the stairs—a hesitant sound, like the person standing at the door really didn't mean to ring it. I felt I might be sick. *This isn't happening.* I looked back at the unmade bed. *If I just crawl back in bed and bring the boys with me . . .* But the doorbell rang again—this time it was persistent—and I was propelled to the stairs which loomed menacingly below me.

I'd left a lamp on for Brian in the foyer. Under it, a frame held a photo of us the day he graduated from the police academy. His crooked smile matched the tilt of his police hat.

On the way home from work that afternoon I picked up more pictures of Brian from our camping trip the week before. At twenty-seven he still looked like a happy kid in his cut-offs and sneakers.

I heard the doorknob rattle and looked down at my nightgown, one reserved for Brian. I leaned against the wall, knowing I could not walk up the stairs for a robe, and let the wall support me as I inched toward the door.

"Kathy, it's Charlie. Open the door, please." He sounded like he had been asking for a long time.

The doorknob didn't seem to work, and I wasn't sure which way to turn the lock. When I finally opened it, I found Charlie standing in front of two men in police uniform. His blue eyes reminded me of Brian's. "You two look like brothers," I had told him when they were assigned to the bomb squad together. Shadows shifted under the porch light, and Charlie looked down to study the flagstones. When he looked up, his eyes were haunted, terrified.

"We lost him."

I shivered uncontrollably. *NO.* I shook my head. *NO.* My legs wouldn't work. *NO.* I looked past Charlie into the street ringed with flashing lights and uniforms.

Charlie tried to lead me to the living room, but I found myself climbing the stairs in a body that felt borrowed from someone else.

Upstairs, the boys' room was still dark. The weight of Chris's sleeping body was almost too heavy to lift, and I sank to the floor with him in my lap. He smelled of baby shampoo and boy sweat. He slept, completely unaware his tiny world would never be the same. Across the room, the nightlight illuminated Keith's deep red hair. I watched his face until he woke up. Sliding off his bed, he sat on the floor beside us. With my free arm I pulled him to my side.

"What's the matter, Mommy?" He had Brian's eyes—those dark, feathery lashes.

"Daddy went to heaven." I didn't recognize my voice.

"How did he get there?"

"God came to get him."

"Can we go see him?"

"Not for a long time, honey." I didn't trust myself to say more.

THE SUN WAS BEGINNING TO rise, its red glow sliding over

blue sailboat wallpaper. It was going to be another hot day. The milk bottles had to go out. Library books were due. *My husband just died,* I would tell the librarian, and thought she might forgive the fine.

Chris woke and blinked sleepily at me. His hair was almost white from the summer sun, his deep green eyes—like mine—were set in a face that called for blue, the difference striking. He put his arms around my neck and buried his face in my shoulder, as though he knew something was wrong.

Keith leaned against me. "Can we have our breakfast now, Mommy?"

The smell of coffee drifted up the stairs as though Brian were in the kitchen, as though it were a normal morning.

A policewoman I had not noticed before was standing in the doorway, and when I rose, she placed a robe over my short nightgown. Chris, big for a two-year-old, slipped from my arms, and she took him from me. Together we made our way down those dizzying stairs to a house full of NYPD.

Cigarette smoke hung in the air. Charlie was sitting in the kitchen, and he stood when he saw me, a cup of black coffee on the table in front of him. Brian's cup. "Hey, Buddy," Charlie called to Keith, who ran into his arms, thinking this an ordinary day, the room full of Daddy's friends.

I felt surrounded by the bombshell I had been handed, disoriented, unable to process the full extent of what happened. The kitchen felt like foreign territory. I fumbled around, looking for Fruit Loops, and poured them into Keith and Chris's *My Pop's a Cop* cereal bowls I made in ceramics class. I told Keith he wouldn't be going to school, that I would call his teacher, and thought of the little nursery classroom we had visited, Brian silly on the tot-sized chair.

"Can I still wear my policeman shirt?" he'd asked.

I looked at Charlie. "Croatians?"

"Yeah. The wife is American, but the cause is for Croatia."

Outside a car door slammed. When I looked out, I saw my mother walking up the driveway, a police officer holding her arm. Her mismatched outfit was out of character for her, as though she had pulled clothes from the closet without looking, her hair slept on. As soon as she was in the door, she called my name, more a sob than a word. She told me once she loved Brian more than me, and I thought of that as she made her way through the living room into the kitchen, where I stood frozen. And then she pulled me into her arms. *These are my mother's arms around me,* I told myself. *Her tears are for me.*

She put her hand on the back of my head. "It will be okay. I'm here." Except that my mother hadn't ever really been there. Growing up, I felt I was just another mouth to feed. Still, as I smelled her Oil of Olay and heard her whisper my name, I let myself collapse into her, and for the first time since Charlie told me Brian had been killed, I cried.

*I wanted to know you moved and
breathed in the same world with me.*
— F. Scott Fitzgerald, *Benediction*

Kathy From The Bronx

1968

McGUINNESS'S ON FLATBUSH WAS PACKED, EVEN FOR A Friday night, the air heavy with cigarette smoke and body heat. Fiona and I squeezed our way through our Brooklyn hangout. It was a dirty old man's bar by day that livened up after work when the Flatbush crowd stopped by for a beer. I had been there when it was near empty and noticed the dirty wood and old Rheingold Beer signs, split leather stools, and mop streaks on worn tiles. It was one of those places that smelled from a lifetime of spilled beer and cigarette smoke, but somehow, when glasses clinked and the jukebox began to pulse, no one seemed to notice.

"Two Dewar's and soda." Fiona flipped her pretty blonde hair and winked at the bartender.

I set my wet wool coat over the back of the stool she was sitting on and leaned against the brass rail. "Hey Jude" blasted through the jukebox, and I thought of Gracie. "Better, Better, Better." I felt the wet snow melting down my back and closed my eyes to send up a silent prayer that my sister, two months free from jail, stayed off drugs, away from Hunts Point and the South Bronx neighborhood that would drag her back down.

"Hey Brian," Fiona shouted over the music. I opened my eyes to see a guy with crazy beautiful eyes staring at me. "Where've you been?"

Brian slowly shifted his eyes from mine to look at her. "How's it going, Fiona?" His navy pea coat was blackened on the shoulders with wet snow.

"I haven't seen you for a long time." Fiona's cheeks, still bright from the cold, flushed even deeper.

"Just home from 'Nam." He glanced at me and then studied his cigarette.

"Welcome home." Fiona leaned over and kissed him on the cheek. "I'm glad you made it back." She sipped her drink.

"What are you having?" He nodded at my glass.

"Dewar's and soda," Fiona said. "This is Kathy, my friend from work. She's from the Bronx."

Brian raised his eyebrows, but he didn't wisecrack about the borough war Dodgers' fans held onto. Instead, his voice was polite, almost formal, "It's nice to meet you Kathy from the Bronx. Did you have a nice Christmas?" Out of the corner of my eye, I saw Fiona turn on her stool to talk to Mike O'Leary.

"It was all right." I fidgeted with the buttons of my blouse, glad I had chosen the soft blue satin, part of my working wardrobe that I paired with a short black skirt and three inch heels. I had been a tall, skinny kid, and now I was a tall, slim woman. My hair curled naturally when it was damp, the color a deep red that had once been the brunt of clown jokes but now turned heads.

"Were you home for Christmas?"

He rubbed his cigarette into the bar ashtray with his thumb, the unfiltered paper reduced to a nub. "For the first time in years." He gave me a half-smile. "And it was great." His body was quiet, exuding a stillness that felt calming.

"How do you know Fiona?" I couldn't look at those eyes, so I studied my red nail polish, shiny in the dim light.

"She went to school with my sister Eileen."

"Hey Kathy." Mike O'Leary had thrown back a few too

many. "I was just telling Fiona here that I won a big trial today." I took a step back from his breath. "I'm celebrating."

"Congratulations," I said. When I turned back, I saw Brian was threading through the crowd to the end of the bar. He stopped briefly to talk to a guy I didn't recognize, shake hands with someone else, and take a quarter out for the jukebox. He signaled to the bartender to order our drinks.

Vietnam. "Fucked up, man," my cousin Frankie had said at his own homecoming a few months back. "Fucked up."

"Oooh, Kathy's got it bad." Fiona's breath was hot in my ear.

"Who is he?" I watched Brian scan the bar while he waited for the drinks. He smiled when he saw me looking.

"He is a sweetheart," Fiona said. "And he cannot stop looking at you." She raised her glass. "Payback for all those Bronx boys you introduced me to." Fiona wasn't like a lot of the gum-smacking girls from Brooklyn. She had spunk, despite the gloominess of the apartment she shared with her mother, who still rolled her hair on a sponge roll, just the way she had as a young girl in Ireland.

Brian's hand brushed mine as he handed me a drink, and I felt him watching me as he sipped from a bottle of Budweiser. His blue pinstriped shirt was open at the collar, and I let my eyes linger on his bare skin. I had one serious boyfriend before, and that was when I was eighteen and thought a twenty-five-year-old attorney named Vincent would deliver to me everything my life was missing. Until I found out he was married with two children.

"Do you have plans for New Years?" he asked.

I nodded, cursing my brother Timmy for making me promise to double-date.

"Last minute." He gave me that half-grin again, and I thought about what it would be like to kiss those lips. "I understand."

The jukebox turned another song. "Hello, I love you, won't you tell me your name. Hello, I love you, let me jump in your game." I could feel the heat crawl up my neck. *Did you play this song?* I wanted to ask him, but he took his last sip of beer and set the bottle on the bar. His eyes never left my face, and I felt like I was swaying on a porch swing dreaming this scene.

"Listen," he said. "My sister is having a family party tonight to welcome me home, so I have to leave, but I would like to see you again some time."

"Fiona and I usually come on Fridays," I said. I was twenty years old and had been coming to McGuinness's for a few years. I was one of the crowd, despite my Bronx address, but had never met anyone here I was drawn to. Until tonight. There were a few admirers, like Richard, who told me how much he loved redheads, or Steve, who thought every woman in McGuinness's was in love with him. But none of them gave me pause the way Brian did.

"Okay." Brian watched me with those eyes. "I'll see you around." He let a moment pass. "But someday I'm going to marry you."

The words didn't sink in for a minute, and before I could say anything Brian was gone. If I wanted to follow him, ask him if he meant what he said, I wouldn't have been able to. I was rooted to the floor, my mind buzzing with his off-hand proposal.

"Air Force." Fiona sidled up next to me. "Last name's Murray, dad has an old man's bar over on Rogers. I'll drive you by his house tomorrow, so you can see where he lives." Suddenly the room was alive with chatter, as though all sound, except for Brian's words, had all fallen away and had just now come back to life.

"WHAT DO YOU THINK ABOUT a guy who says he's going to marry me the first time we meet?"

My boss, Harry Banks, and I were having lunch in his office. His pastrami sandwich was too big for his mouth, but he shoveled it in anyway. I piled half my pastrami on the deli wrapper. "I'll take the rest of that." He reached over with his fork. "I would say he likes you." Harry was the president of Hamilton

Adams, an Irish import company, where I worked as his administrative assistant. Most of the office was terrified of his short fuses and endless demands. But I witnessed worse in my own father and found it easy, almost familiar, to be with him.

"He is a friend of Fiona's. Just discharged from the Air Force." I wanted to tell him about Brian's eyes, the swept-up way he had of looking at me.

"So, what's the problem?" Harry opened his second bag of chips.

"The problem is he said someday he would marry me." The thought still made my legs weak.

"Yeah, well," Harry wiped his mouth with his napkin. "He is either in love or crazy. Take it slow."

"I will," I said. But I couldn't stop thinking about him.

During the day, I showed Irish linen samples to fashion design showrooms, took inventory, and sent telex correspondence to our mills in Belfast. At five o'clock, I took the subway home to the tiny Throggs Neck apartment where my mother, and five of my seven brothers and sisters and I fought for space. The noise was constant—the patter of footsteps, raised and hushed voices, the ever-present din of televisions all set to different programs. It was a step up from where we came from—a basement apartment in the South Bronx—but still, the crowded space left plenty of room to long for a tiny slice of privacy.

In a tight back bedroom, my sister Gracie and I slept in twin beds, our nightstand piled high with books. Even walking the streets when she was using drugs, she always had a book with her, and we passed them back and forth, precious, like keys to another life. It wasn't long before Brian became woven into that make-believe world that carried me away from Randall Avenue. My prince in a pea coat.

"So, what's he look like?" Gracie lay on her back with her eyes closed when I told her how he bought me a drink and then disappeared into the snow, right after he said he was going to marry me. Gracie smiled, as if proud. She had always kept me pretty. While my little sister and brothers ran wild, dirty from playing in the cellar, Gracie washed my face and combed my hair. Watching me walk up the cement steps from our basement apartment like a peacock, her response was always the same. "You look beautiful," she would say.

I told her how Fiona and I drove by his house, a brownstone with stained glass windows, a little manicured lawn, the works.

After that, every time the phone rang, Gracie asked, "Was that him?"

And just when I thought I would never hear from him again, she left a message on my pillow. *Brian Murray. BU 8-2784.* The old rotary dial took forever to circle, sluggishly settling back into place before I could rotate the dial again for the next number.

He answered on the second ring, his voice deep, husky. "I'm glad you called back," he said.

I pictured that smile, had already memorized it when I closed my eyes and thought about the night I met him. "Did Fiona give you my number?"

"No, my sister Eileen knows where Fiona works, and I called for your last name and looked you up in the phone book."

"What are you, a detective?" My own smile looked goofy in the hall mirror. The phone sat on a tin folding table where everyone could hear your conversation.

"Not yet, but I'm waiting for the next class to join the NYPD. I'll be a detective one day."

"You'll make a good one." I whispered the words, keeping Brian close, away from my depressing Bronx apartment.

"How about dinner Saturday night?" he asked.

"I would like that," I said, and after we hung up I stood for a long time staring at the phone. I wanted to call him back. *I've been thinking about you,* I wanted to tell him. *I can't stop.*

SATURDAY, SLEET RAPPED THE WINDOWPANE, blurring the apartment building across the street. *He won't come in this weather,* I kept thinking. I read the same paragraph of Arthur Hailey's *Airport* twice without remembering it. Fingering the little bumps on my chenille bedspread, I watched Gracie look for something to wear in the dresser drawers. Rich red hair and high cheekbones like Katherine Hepburn, she had been clean since Bedford Hills, where she did eighteen months for drug possession. "What happened to the closet?" She touched the split wood around the lock. We kept the closet locked and barricaded against our brother, Corky, who sold anything not nailed down for drugs. I saw right away when she opened the door that the top shelf was empty. I dropped the book.

"My camera."

Gracie narrowed her eyes. "That son-of-a-bitch."

"I hocked it." Corky was sitting on the living room couch flipping through the TV Guide, his voice defiant.

My ears rang. "What do you mean you hocked it?"

He got up. "Hocked." He was six inches taller than me. "Are you deaf?"

When I took a swing at him he caught my hand with his forearm. Pain shot up to my shoulder, and I backed away just in time to miss his punch. Gracie held him back, finally pushing him out the door, almost tipping over the china cabinet, where the Waterford crystal shook and then steadied.

To breathe through the pain, I sat on the plastic-covered couch and studied the Waterford toasting flutes and vases, an ashtray that never held ashes, the crystal that was my mother's pride and joy. Her friend Simone worked shipping at Bloomingdales and kept sending pieces "by mistake" to the Bronx instead of Westchester. "I think he broke my hand," I told Gracie. It was already beginning to swell.

"Come on, Mom won't be home from work for a few hours. I'll take you to the hospital."

Instead of the bus, we pooled our money for a cab. The driver sang along to "Love Child" on his radio. Outside, the sleet came down sideways, freezing rain that coated the streets. Gracie blew smoke through a little crack in the window. I thought about when my father finished boxing my mother around, how he used to torture Corky, beat him with a broomstick, a belt, his fists.

"We need to get him out," I said now. My hand throbbed.

"Fat chance," Gracie said. "You think Mom has any control over him?"

"You shouldn't be around him. He's bad news, too much temptation." In fact, Gracie hated Corky almost as much as I did and kept as far away from him as she could. But they had been looking for the same fix on the streets for years, and I was pretty sure if Gracie decided to get high, Corky would have no problem bringing her back into the using fold.

AFTER FIVE HOURS IN AN emergency room that smelled like sewer, and X-rays that showed a hairline fracture, they fit me for a cast.

My mother was at the kitchen table when we got home, *The Daily News* spread out in front of her, next to a glass ashtray of crushed Pall Malls stained by her red lipstick. "How do you spell method?" Patrick asked her.

"M-E-T-Haitch-O-D." Her parents' Irish accents were still noticeable.

I stood in front of her with my cast.

"What?" she asked.

"Throw Corky out or I'm gone." This wasn't the first time I wore a cast or sported a black eye from a fight with him. She had served as Corky's punching bag herself. I was twenty years old, earned a decent salary, contributed to the rent, and yet my mother still did not hear me.

She picked up her cigarettes without looking at me. "I'll talk to him." She stood. The run in her nylons showed varicose veins that mapped her once-beautiful legs. I watched her cross the room and thought of her at sixteen, walking home from Cardinal Spellman, boys stealing looks. I knew where she was going. She would close the door to her bedroom and tune us out, imagine herself elsewhere, anywhere except trapped in this tiny, crowded apartment with the eternal televisions, footsteps coming and going at all hours, where everyone wanted something from her.

"He's here," Gracie called from the window.

I looked down at my old dungarees, a wrinkled t-shirt of my brother Timmy's I had thrown on before we went out the door. "Jesus," I told her. "I'm a mess."

"Quick." Gracie pushed me toward the bedroom, her eyes two sparks. "Go change. I'll keep him company."

Nothing fit over the cast. Finally, I found a red sweater with stretched-out sleeves and matched it to a short black skirt. Heels were out of the question with the icy streets, so I settled for my furry boots, and then studied myself in the mirror hanging from the closet Corky had jimmied open. It wasn't how I wanted to look for my first date with a man who said he would marry me. I tried to fix my splotchy face with make-up, but my right hand was useless. My hair was a nest of tangles, and when I tried to comb it, the frizz won. Finally, I walked out the bedroom door.

"The roads are slippery," I heard Brian say to Gracie. "But I made it in an hour."

I tried to hear what Gracie said back, but the TV drowned out her voice. It had been a long time since I had introduced Gracie to my friends. I didn't want Brian to know she was twenty-eight, had been messed up since she was eighteen, still shared my room, and that was the good part. Her husband was in jail, her sons parceled out. I wouldn't know how to explain that even strung-out on drugs, she had always been a mother to me, and that had grounded her. Now, we grounded each other. *I probably won't see him again,* I thought as I walked toward the living room. *He'll think we are violent or crazy.*

Timmy, Danny, and Patrick were watching TV and ignored Brian. He sat in the same spot Corky had sat in hours before, and he stood when I came in the room. His smile faded as he took in the cast.

"Hey," he said. He was wearing a cream button-down Oxford and a gold watch that looked like a graduation gift.

"Hi." I headed for the door. "There's a restaurant a few blocks away."

"Nice to meet you, Gracie," he said over his shoulder. He followed me down four flights of stairs that smelled like a dirty mop. On the last step my foot caught, and I felt his hand on my arm.

"Hey." That same husky voice. "Slow down." His suede jacket, spotted dark in places from the sleet, smelled like rich leather, and I wanted to rest my head against his chest and stay there forever. "We're in no rush." He placed my coat over my shoulders and held my elbow as we walked along the sidewalk slick with ice.

His white Volkswagen looked brand new. It was parked a few cars down from the car I shared with Timmy, an old Nash Rambler convertible with no back window and a hole in the floor near the accelerator. I waited while he opened the door for me. Inside, it was quiet and warm.

His hair seemed longer than it had at the bar, more civilian, and he was sporting new sideburns. The windshield wipers shuddered as they cleared a small circle in the ice. "Daydream Believer" played on the radio, and he turned and gave me that half-grin. "Where to?" he asked.

I directed him right, then left. "I thought you might cancel because of the storm." The moon was a soft glow on the streets' glistening surfaces. "I'm glad you didn't."

"I wanted to see you." He glanced at me. "Weather wouldn't stop me."

I wanted to say something back, tell him how happy I was, but the pill the doctor had given me at the hospital had worn off and pain was beginning to drill through my hand.

Orlando's smelled like garlic and was empty, save one other couple brave enough to come out in the weather. "Good evening, Kathy," the hostess, Marie, a friend of my mother's, greeted us. Her eyes widened when she saw the cast, but she knew enough not to ask questions. "Miserable night out isn't it?" She seated us and handed us menus.

"Marie, meet Brian." She gave him a quick up and down.

When we were alone she would want the details, but she was working now and polite. I knew she would tell my mother everything as soon as she had the chance.

"Nice to meet you," Brian said.

I took my time with the menu. At home I let the boys have first run at the leftovers my mother brought us home from the automat.

"What happened to your hand?" Brian asked.

"I had a fight with my—" but I felt the hot sting of tears and quit talking.

"It's all right." He looked at me over his menu. "I have sisters."

I wasn't sure what he meant, but it made me laugh. "So do I." I wiped my eyes on the napkin. "And four brothers too."

"Well, you beat me there. I have one brother."

"I got in a fight with one of them," I said quickly. "He stole my camera. He'll steal anything he can sell."

Brian watched me. He was quiet for a while. Finally, he passed me the bread. "I think I'll have the steak," he said, saving me from talking about Corky. "You?" He aligned his knife and fork with the plate.

"I'll have the same." I smiled

"How about a bottle of Pinot Noir?"

I wasn't sure what kind of wine Pinot Noir was, but it sounded perfect.

When Marie brought our meals, I realized I couldn't cut my meat. Brian reached over and took the knife from my hand. His forehead creased while he cut, and I could smell the wine, those Lucky Strikes that reminded me of Gracie, and the leather from his suede jacket.

"When are you going on the police force?" I took a sip of the wine and rolled it around in my mouth.

He glanced at me. "I'm not sure. With Mayor Lindsay's

layoffs, it might not be for a while."

"How do you know you'll be called?"

He cut the meat into precise, bite-size pieces. "They already interviewed me. I worked with munitions in the Air Force."

"Munitions?"

"Military weapons. Bombs."

I studied the strong flex of his jaw. "Isn't that scary?"

"No. It isn't the kind of job you can do if you're scared." He cut the last bite of steak. "It takes a steady hand."

"You must have nerves of steel." *And the longest lashes I have ever seen on a guy.*

"There aren't too many ways to wire a bomb." He put the knife and fork down. "So once you know the circuitry, it's just a matter of steady hands and a lot of patience." He settled back into his seat.

"So, as a cop, you would take apart bombs?"

"That's the plan."

I looked down at my plate and felt the excitement of the direction his life would take, and wondered if I would be part of it, if he really meant it when he said he wanted to marry me.

"Actually, would you cut the broccoli, too?"

"Pleasure's all mine." He started cutting again.

Over dinner, he poured my wine, told me he was building garages until he could start at the academy, said he had a brother who was a state trooper and married, with a little girl. He had three sisters. One was married with a baby, another took care of the third sister who had Down syndrome. Their alcoholic mother couldn't take care of herself.

"But my father," he said, "is a great guy who does his best to hold things together."

He tugged at his new sideburns while he talked. When he asked about my family I dodged his questions. The ones I couldn't dodge, I answered carefully, filtering my replies. But eventually the wine loosened me up, and I found myself telling him about how my mother was the manager of the Horn & Hardart on 59th, across from Bloomingdales, and about my father leaving when I was a kid. While we talked, the wax dripped off the candles in the Chianti bottle holders, their flames flickering every time Marie walked past; Brian told me he liked my hair, loved my smile, asked did I want more wine? He asked if my steak was okay. Did my hand hurt? He said since we met at McGuinness's, he was pretty sure not one minute had gone by when he wasn't thinking about me. With each question, I fell a little more in love.

It was still sleeting when we left the restaurant, and Brian drove slowly the few blocks to the apartment. With the car idling we talked until three in the morning. When I looked up again, the sleet had stopped, and the trees sparkled like silver prisms.

"Would you like to go to the Bronx Zoo next Sunday?"

The Bronx Zoo was my favorite. Growing up, I took the bus there weekly to get away from home. "All right."

His kiss was soft, and we lingered for just a moment before he whispered in my ear, "Good night, Kathy from the Bronx."

I have spread my dreams under your feet;
Tread softly because you tread on my dreams.
— W. B. Yeats, Aedh Wishes for
the Cloths of Heaven

Not Suitable For Viewing

1976

BACK IN OUR DARKENED BEDROOM, I FELT SAFE FROM THE forlorn looks of my family and friends that threatened to send me over the edge. Lying in bed, I could still feel him with me, the heat of his body, the faint scent of his lime shaving cream on the sheets. *I'll never wash them.* I remembered buying the bedroom set seven years ago when we were first married and thought we would sleep in this bed for a lifetime.

Now I closed my eyes and felt the vibration from downstairs where top brass from the department Brian had devoted his life to were making plans to bury him.

My mother brought me tea and toast. I hardly recognized her. Growing up, she had been elusive, always trying to pull herself away from our neediness. She was an empty nester now, still living in the Bronx, but without eight children in tow, free for the first time in her life. The mothering that had lain dormant all those years suddenly emerged now, in the aftermath of Brian's death. She sat by my bed and wiped my face with a washcloth and held my hand while I slept, as though caring for me had come naturally all her life, making me forget the little girl who'd begged her for scraps of love all those years ago.

An NYPD doctor tried to give me tranquilizers, but I was afraid of drugs, afraid I would drown in them like Gracie and never resurface. During my fitful attempts to sleep, dreams of Brian tormented me. I dreamed of my father's dark street in Brooklyn, crowded with rows of dilapidated apartments with slumped wooden stoops, aligned railroad style, one bedroom the entrance to another, without any privacy. The child-sized bathroom was an afterthought, the kitchen windows nailed shut to keep out the Bushwick Avenue junkies. His piles of paperback crime novels were stacked around the room knee-high, serving as makeshift tables holding filled ashtrays. I could see a blue light under the door, but as I moved into the next room, the light vanished and slipped under the door into the room beyond, and then again until there were no more rooms. I opened the last door to find Brian sitting in a faded red wing chair, his hands on the dirty armrests. The right side of his face was as I remembered him, but parts of the left side hung off, like the stuffing of the chair. "They want me to disappear for a while," I heard him say. "So the terrorists get the death penalty. It's the only way." He filled the room and I breathed him in, floating toward him, so relieved to have him back. His injuries didn't matter. I would heal him. But when I reached out, he vanished.

I tried to fight off my mother's voice, but I woke to sweltering heat and sat up, confused. In the bathroom, I lay on the cool tile, too weak to lift my head, the room spinning. I noticed a slight film around the bathtub where I had let out the water just a few days ago, when I'd bathed in blissful ignorance, my world still intact, before the pall that now hung over the house showed even in the eyes of my little boys.

"Let me run a shower for you," my mother said. I watched her prepare a towel and washcloth. She washed my hair like I was a little girl again, as if it had been her, and not Gracie, who had taken care of me then. "God, you're so thin," she mumbled.

Who cares? Who will ever care? I let the wall hold me up. She came back with a black dress I had never seen. "Gracie bought this for you. You need to be at the wake tonight. Everyone wants to know where you are." *Gracie*, I thought. *The only one I want to be with.*

Looking around the bedroom now, it seemed incredible that nothing had changed. My mother had pulled the curtain closed, leaving a crack of light where the harsh sun slanted across Brian's closet—a crude reminder of the suits he wore to work that were still on credit. On his dresser was a mahogany jewelry box with a pair of cufflinks inherited from his father, a crumpled five-dollar bill, loose change, a napkin with the name Rob, and a 212 phone number written in Brian's slanted handwriting. His khaki slacks, flung across a chair, were frayed at the back pocket where he kept his shield. I picked up the pants and in the front pocket found a book of matches from the Market Diner in Hell's Kitchen where he sometimes had dinner with Charlie. I folded them over a hanger and added them to the row of khakis in his closet the way he would have, if he were still here.

By his own admission, Brian was a neat freak, organization he said he brought back from his military days when he shined his shoes until they were mirrors and folded his clothes precisely. It was a trait I clearly lacked, my clothes on wire hangers smooshed together in the bigger closet Brian let me have all to myself.

Compromise was a big part of our marriage. We divided household chores, Brian the better cook, I the shopper and scrubber of toilets. I put in as many work hours as he did in the beginning of our marriage. After Keith, and twenty-one months later, when Chris was born, I reduced my time to anywhere from three to five days a week, from nine until two, so I could be home in time for Brian to leave for his steady four-to-twelves, with rotating days off. We had even compromised on the names we choose for our children. "You get to name girls," he had said, "and I get to name boys."

FOR THE FIRST TIME SINCE the doorbell rang two nights before I glanced at my reflection in the mirror. I had become a shadow. The green eyes Brian had loved held an emotion he'd never seen, a new anger, a cold rage, and I didn't recognize the person in them. I would never feel his body again. My sons would never know their father. I could feel the erosion of trust I had built with Brian and realized I had lost the life I had spent my whole life waiting for.

Downstairs, everyone I knew seemed to be in the living room, stepping around the polished hardwood floors Brian and I had discovered hidden under worn carpet. We found this Rockville Centre house right before Keith was born. Brian knocked down walls and finished the basement, and we spent years making the house our own.

Now the house was crowded with police officers who stood talking about losing one of their brothers. It no longer felt like ours. Thankfully Brian's parents were both dead, saving me from having to deal with his alcoholic mother and sweet-natured father who would be crushed by the death of his boy.

"Mommy!" Keith left the Candy Land game he and his cousin had been playing and ran to me.

"Mommy's okay, sweetie." I bent down to hug him, and his arms squeezed with all the might of a four-year-old.

"Come give Mommy a hug, Chris." My youngest pushed aside *Goodnight Moon* and slipped off the couch. I blinked away tears. I had to be strong for them.

On my way to the kitchen, I passed my neighbor. "Terrorists?" she asked, her eyes red and swollen. I shook my head, unable to give her an answer.

Annie closed the refrigerator door and looked up, surprised to see me. My younger sister had been making sandwiches, ever the efficient and organized one. Rose stood at the sink washing dishes and gave me a sad smile when she saw me. "You okay?" All I could do was nod. The oldest of our sprawling family, she might have been composed up to that point, but when she grabbed me in a tight hug I could feel her quiet sobs.

I couldn't cry with her. If I did, I would never stop. My mother sat at the kitchen table with the red-checkered tablecloth staring out the window. Gracie was standing next to her, and after meeting my eyes, she led me back through the living room where my brother Timmy sat alone in a chair, his hands braced on the armrests. I stopped for a moment to kiss his cheek, drained and ghostly white, and I remembered Charlie said it was Timmy who identified Brian's body. Outside, my brothers Danny and Patrick were on the front porch, smoking. I was grateful Corky had stayed away.

In our bedroom, a place where I could curl up and disappear, I began to process what I knew thus far. Brian removed the bomb from a locker and brought it to the range. Then what? The implications of his next steps settled in my stomach like acid. Did he cross wires? Was it his fault? The idea was impossible to imagine.

THE AIR IN THE POLICE car was hot and close. My mother and Gracie sat on either side of me. "The dress is too big on you," Gracie said, taking a cigarette out of her pack. She looked pale, her short-sleeved dress revealing slight track marks running up her wrists. She was clean as a whistle now, and not going back, she said. When I reached over to roll down the window, she patted my arm. "No handles in squad cars." She lit her cigarette. "I should know." She leaned over and put her match in the steel ashtray. "First ride in one of these without handcuffs."

My mother kept her eyes on the two escort cars ahead, parting traffic on Clinton Avenue, which was normally quiet.

"I don't want to see those uniforms." I looked at the Rockville Centre police cars lining the street. "It hurts to look at them."

Gracie leaned against the window and closed her eyes. "Tell me about it."

With its white clapboards and green shutters, Macken

Mortuary looked more like the colonials that lined the streets of Rockville Centre than a funeral parlor. I'd driven by it a hundred times and never given it a second thought. But now, my husband was lying in a coffin inside one of the rooms.

I looked out at the line snaking down the sidewalk and around the block. It surprised me, as I hadn't thought about anyone else mourning him. His death belonged to me alone, to our sons.

We parked in the back next to a Mercy Hospital ambulance. "So you can go in without having to pass all those people," my mother explained, adjusting the pearls around her neck.

"Why is the ambulance here?" I asked the police officer when he opened my door.

He didn't meet my eyes. "In case someone needs medical attention." *Me,* I thought. *They mean me.*

Through the back door and down the long hallway, my mother and Gracie held onto me. The tinny smell of the air-conditioning came through the vents and goose bumps stood out on my arms. We stopped at a side doorway and looked in at the dimly lit room. The accordion walls had been folded back so it was double in size, but the crowd and the hundreds of flower arrangements made it appear small. My family and Brian's were in clusters near the coffin. Two military guards in decorated uniforms stood sentry over the shining wooden box. A police officer kept the line moving past the coffin, as though directing traffic on some crowded thoroughfare. The coffin was closed. "Why?" I asked my mother.

She squeezed my hand. "They didn't want you to see him."

That rage arrived again, titanic and almost unbearably restless. "I don't care what he looks like." I tried to control my voice. "I want to see his face again."

"He's wearing his police uniform and his wedding ring," she said. My mother held fast to my arm as though I might run from her. Does that mean his body was in one piece? I wanted to ask. Or shredded and mutilated?

When we first began to date, I thought Brian would realize

his mistake and stop driving to the Bronx. I told him my darkest secrets, about my brother, my father, my mother, and confessed that I didn't think I knew how to love. But he didn't shy away from those stories, and instead told me of his own dark memories, of a mother who only played at her role in the presence of his father, of the military assignment to assemble explosives, of the Vietnamese children he met on bike rides through villages, innocent of the torn-up country around them. He wanted to do something for them, he told me, of the village children who all looked alike in the grainy photos he kept in his desk drawer, with dusty shorts and bare feet. So he brought candy just to see their faces light up at the surprise Hershey bar. He confessed that he dreamed about the families whose lives could be obliterated by the bombs he assembled.

"You feel that?" Gracie whispered. A palpable ripple went through the room, as though a slight wind had caught the crowd. "They just realized you're standing here." And that's when I understood I wasn't invisible. All my life I felt invisible. It was one of the things that had drawn me to Brian—that he actually saw me, all of me. And now, standing in that room, I realized that everyone was looking at me. On the one day I wanted to be hidden from view, I had become the most conspicuous person in the room—The Widow.

"Come." My mother touched my arm and led me into the room.

Dennis, Brian's older brother, looked down at me with those blue eyes so much like Brian's. "How you doing?" His square jaw flexed over and over again. A man's grief was different, tense and secretive. Dennis was an FBI agent and Brian had looked up to him, followed his footsteps and joined the Air Force, then went into law enforcement.

Dennis gave me a sturdy hug, and I felt myself collapse into him. Over his shoulder, I watched his sister crying. "He was crazy about you," Dennis said into my hair. I nodded. It was hard to look at Eileen, who could have been Brian's twin. "Hey sweetie." She came over and hugged and kissed me, dabbing at her eyes, and then mine, with her handkerchief. "Us Brian lovers have to stick together." Her voice was deep, exhausted. "He was our hero."

The fifteen remaining men on the bomb squad stood in a close-shouldered group by the wall. When I looked over at them, they seemed to study the floor or each other's shoes, as if they were afraid to speak to me. When I started to walk toward them, Paul Eckelmann and Bobby Tellone left a group of police uniforms and came over.

"You okay?" Paul folded me in his arms. A six-foot-four teddy bear, I felt tiny next to him. He and Bobby were at the academy with Brian. We danced at their weddings, celebrated the birth of their children. "Hold on there, Kat." Bobby took my other arm. I thought if they let go, I would fall down. "The room's clean," Paul waved his arm toward the crowded room. "Swept of weapons. Bomb dogs called it safe." I nodded mechanically. *Safe. Bomb dogs.*

As we approached the bomb squad, only Charlie stepped forward to greet me. Odd, because these men were family. Charlie's familiar eyes had a hardness to them, as though part stone, and he held me by the shoulders instead of hugging me, keeping me at arm's length. "We're all broken up he's gone." I saw his blonde hair had been freshly cut, marine short. It framed a face that looked paler, even, than the night he rang the doorbell. I nodded, and, for one stinging moment, I hated his wife for still having a husband.

Hank Dworkin put his hand out to me, his face covered in red welts where the shrapnel had hit him. He squeezed my fingers.

"How did it happen?" I asked Hank. I hadn't planned to ask. Inspector Behr, commander of the bomb squad unit, stepped between us.

"Brian was a hero." He said it defensively and then glanced around, his deep-set eyes shadowed by a pair of darkened glasses. "Admired by everyone who knew him." He took my hand from Hank and held it, his lips disappearing when he smiled.

"How is Terry McTigue?" I tried to get my hand free from Behr.

Charlie glanced at Hank, who ran his fingers around his shirt collar. "Severe injuries." Behr slowly shook his head. "But he's alive." I had a swift vision of Terry in that coffin instead of Brian.

"The mayor is here." Charlie nodded to Behr. "He wants a few words with her."

Paul took my hand from Behr, and he and Bobby led me to a group of police who surrounded Mayor Beam. "You have our deepest regrets." The mayor had an air of confidence some short men have and reminded me of my boss Harry. "If there is anything you need just call my office." His pink scalp peeked through strands of hair.

"Thank you, Mr. Mayor." *Thank you?* I watched him continue toward where the real brass was, where Commissioner Codd lingered.

"What does he look like?" I asked Paul as we moved toward the coffin.

Paul glanced over my head at Bobby. "The truth? Not suitable for viewing."

Not suitable for viewing. Not suitable for viewing. The words echoed dully in my head as I stood staring at the coffin. Dozens of white roses surrounded the words *Beloved Father*. After a moment, I felt Paul and Bobby moving me to the right like a stand-up doll, so the people circling the room and passing the casket could begin to greet me.

"There's the bomb squad from Germany." Paul motioned to the line that had begun to move toward me. I remembered when Brian traveled to FBI headquarters in Quantico to collaborate with the German bomb squad on their newest techniques, how I had missed him but knew then he would come home.

I was a standing zombie, greeting one after another as they

came with the same words. Sorry for your loss, sorry for your loss, so sorry, pain clouding their eyes, as though what was good and wholesome in this world had been smashed to pieces. I looked to them for solace, but what I saw was incomprehension. We were all thinking the same thing: Why did this happen?

Finally, Father Donnelly arrived. "I would like to talk to you in private." He smoothed his cassock and glanced at the crowd. "To go over the sermon for tomorrow."

On the way out I saw my father leaning against the wall near the door. He looked shrunken, his face a gray mass of wrinkles. The suit he wore was too big for him, its elbows and knees shiny from wear. A solitary figure, he was a man who fathered eight children he didn't love. My husband had been the only person in the family who was ever kind to him, and I recalled when Brian insisted we invite my father to our Brooklyn apartment for dinner, and how I resisted. "But he's your father," Brian had said, and I relented, but hated every minute of the awkward evening and never used the iron he brought as a gift.

From the outside, it looked like Brian had a much better life. There were no heroin needles on his sidewalks, no spray-painted gang symbols on the walls of his Brooklyn brownstone. His father owned Ray Murray's bar, and provided for his five children. But his mother was an alcoholic, and although they had financial means, she was erratic, and sometimes downright crazy.

Brian's father died from a heart attack on a cold January day, and when the furnace ran out of oil, lay frozen on the living room couch for days before Brian found him. He didn't know how long his father had been dead or how long his mother stayed in the freezing house with her husband's body.

His mother died seven months later, and again, Brian discovered the body. Liver damage, the coroner told him. When we cleaned out her house we found clothing with tags still attached, long outgrown, toys never played with, and thousands of Green Stamps now stuck together. The attic was filled with enough crystal, silver, and china to open a shop. Aubusson rugs were trussed and shoved under antique furniture, all covered with years of dust. She was a collector, a talented one. She just couldn't share what she collected.

Father Donnelly ushered me out of the reception room. I was thankful to leave behind the overpowering scent of flowers and followed him down a hallway with several doors marked Private. Behind those doors I pictured quiet offices with tufted chairs where families sat to make funeral arrangements. He turned the knob to the one of the doors and I stood in the dark room, exhaustion blanketing me in a thick wave, and listened as he fiddled for the light switch. When the room brightened I realized it was not an office, but a preparation room. The body of an old gray man lay on a table, small and thin like my father. Then I saw a rush of black, and I felt myself falling. The next thing I heard were the sirens racing me to the hospital in the ambulance I had seen waiting.

*Behind all your stories is always your mother's
story because hers is where yours begins.*
— Mitch Albom, *For One More Day*

Faile Street

Everything Brian represented died with him— safety, strength, life without fear. After we met and married, he had saved me from years of living in cramped tenement apartments, and, in the deepest part of me, I worried I would fall back into that poverty, and somehow my boys would slide into the hardship that I'd experienced as a child. I had been too young to understand that my father's leaving brought the shift into poverty, and along with it, a Faile Street address with spidery hallways, dumbwaiters, and a chain toilet.

The walls of the Faile Street alleyways belonged to the Crypts and Diablos—stabbings and gang wars as constant as the sirens along Bruckner Boulevard. At first, our building had seemed a kind of oasis, with gleaming marble steps that led to, what seemed to my young eyes, a palatial lobby adorned with a chandelier and mirrored walls. But then, our mother led us to the basement where we would live as janitors. Long pipes ran across ceilings, the walls were coated with black soot. We made ten trips down to the basement, toting our clothes stuffed into pillowcases in the flexible flyer we'd used to bring our belongings to our new address. The steps were so steep we had to slide against the wall to keep from breaking our necks.

A thin slice of watery sunlight peeked through the kitchen

window, and I could see outside where old snow piled up against the building, thawed and refrozen, and then dulled by city dust.

"I can manage here without having to pay rent," my mother said as we stood around waiting for her to tell us what to do. But she stared ahead like we weren't even there, her eyes transfixed on a cockroach crawling on the stove. She hadn't put on stockings even though it was cold out, and the veins in her feet looked like blue lightning.

My mother, Sarah Martin, was thirty-five in 1954, overweight, and the mother of eight. She didn't have any money, but she had a job and a rent-free apartment, and she was finally rid of a husband who had blackened her eyes and knocked out her teeth for nineteen years.

"I'm going to smash in Dad's head with this baseball bat if he comes back," Corky said to no one, holding onto the bat he used for little league.

"It stinks in here. I want to go home," I cried to my mother, reaching for her hand. Home had been an apartment on Hoe Avenue, sunshiny bright, where you could watch the world from the window seat.

My mother took her hand from mine and brushed crumbs off a red Formica table. "This is home." Yellow stuffing poked out from chairs that someone left behind. A flattened garbage can cover and an empty box of Nabisco crackers littered the floor.

In a small back bedroom where an alleyway blocked out the sun, I watched my mother smooth sheets across her bed, and then she closed the door and turned the lock. I stood outside her door calling her name until Gracie took me by the hand. "Let her rest," she said.

Gracie let me sleep in her bed that first night in the basement on Faile Street. She painted my nails pink, and read to me a chapter from *The Good Earth*, a book we had begun on Hoe Avenue, about Chinese people whose lives seemed much worse than ours. I wondered if that was why she had chosen it, to make us feel better than those poor people in the story. The next morning, Gracie cleaned up the bathroom so we could all take baths, and then swept up the garbage in the cellar so it wouldn't smell so bad.

"Stay away from the boiler room," my mother warned me, but, of course, I had to peek into the room that held a giant furnace where flames licked the iron door. It was my mother who fed that furnace coal, answered the tenants' bells when the water wasn't hot enough, mopped the marble steps from the roof down. I was too young to understand that my mother couldn't tend to me then because she was exhausted from dragging behind her a baggage-load of broken dreams.

Once upon a time my mother had been redheaded, blue eyed, lusciously curved, in love with a boy from the neighborhood. It was her own father who had forced her to marry Tom Martin, my father, twelve years her senior.

"I need you to be a big girl for me," she would tell me, but I didn't want to be a big girl. I wanted her.

"Do you love me Mommy?"

"If I didn't love you, I would give you away."

"Who would you give me to?"

"Don't worry. No one wants you."

She didn't have time to love one child with seven more pulling on her skirts, and I was never the good little girl, my frizzy red hair and freckled face weren't cute enough. When anyone cooed over the five little ones, their smile faded when they came to me. My second-grade picture showed bangs zigzagging across my forehead, barrettes at opposite angles. I wasn't smiling. I was afraid of everything, bums who loitered in the alleyways with their brown paper bags of whiskey, loud noises, cats, dogs, boogymen who were always waiting to pounce.

In my play-cave on Faile Street I hid under the covers, waiting for my mother to wonder where I was. My cave was a sheet tied over the top bunk bed. From it I could see into the living room where Danny ran in circles around the coffee table.

Blue safety pins that held up his diaper peeked through a hole in his rubber pants. I watched him pick up the glass ashtray, almost too heavy for his small hands, raise it over his head, and drop it into the cradle where Patrick was sleeping. Patrick's screams brought my mother in. When she found Danny trying to climb into the cradle, she backhanded him.

"Damn you all to hell!" she screamed.

She picked up the ashtray and cigarette butts from the cradle and wiped Patrick's face with the end of her flowered apron. Then she sat down on the couch that made a whooshing sound, took a Pall Mall from her apron pocket, lit a match, and tossed it near the ashtray. She left her two sons, seventeen months apart, to cry it out, never once glancing my way.

The only time I had my mother to myself was when I made myself wake up early. Taking my spot on the edge of the claw-foot tub, I would watch her put on makeup, trying to cover up the bruises my father left when he showed up in a drunken rage. Like an artist, she put on a layer of pancake makeup over a dark spot on her cheek and let it dry, and then went back and applied another coat until I could hardly detect the black and blue.

She had wavy red hair like Gracie and me, lots of curves, and long muscular legs. I watched her roll up her stockings and look over her shoulder to make sure the seams lined up. "Are they on straight?" she would ask. I backed up, scrutinizing the seams like they were plumb lines. "A little crooked," I would tell her, but in truth I just wanted to see her roll the silk down her thigh, feel for the seam, and roll it back up again.

It was our time together, the morning ritual of watching her dress for work in her pink and brown uniform and white apron. Those were the only times we talked like mother and daughter, and she would sometimes tell me stories about growing up one of four sisters, just like me. But once the day started, it was as if I became invisible, one of eight children who all wanted something from her, even if it was something important, like education.

I OFTEN SAT ON THE stoop to watch kids line up across the street at P.S. 75. Kids in our building who were my age had parents who combed their hair and dressed them up and held their hand as they crossed the street. I wanted desperately to join them for what Gracie told me was kindergarten. I pleaded with my mother, but all she would say is "next year." Next year, she said, I could go into first grade, but I wanted to go now, so I asked Gracie.

"Why can't I go to kindergarten?"

And my thirteen-year-old sister heard me. "Because you need special clothes for school, and Mommy doesn't have the money to buy them." She gave my hand a squeeze. "Let me see if I can dig something up for you."

And just as she promised, Gracie garnered some old hand-me-down school dresses. I was in love with those dresses even though one was a red plaid made of wool that itched so badly my stomach was raw from scratching. Another was a pink, frilly party dress with crinolines that made the bottom stick out and my brothers laugh, but I didn't care. While my mother went to work and my siblings ran around the basement, Gracie combed my hair into a ponytail for my first day of school.

School had been in session for a month, but for me, everything was brand new. The classroom smelled of wax and freshly sharpened pencils. The ABCs and 123s that Gracie had already taught me surrounded the room. I sat behind Angela from 4B, whose last name started with L. Both Angela's parents were teachers, and she looked like she had been born in the schoolroom. She was wearing light blue ribbons in her hair. "They match my eyes," she told me when we lined up. Across from me was just plain Jay, as the kids in our building called him because his brothers were James and Joseph. He was wearing a white shirt and tie, his usual unruly hair smoothed across his head, a miniature of his father.

Every face in the room was familiar, Laura from 3C, whose mother ironed for Jay's. Arthur, whose mother fed him so much that his kindergarten clothes strained at the seams. Bobby, whose mother was a janitor like mine, wore his older brother's white shirt with grayed cuffs, the toes of his shoes scuffed from dragging his feet.

Mrs. Rosen's heavy black glasses hid her eyes, her thick heels echoed through the room. No one talked as she walked up and down the aisle, inspecting our drawings. "Now you will be examined by the nurse," she said when she got to the front of the class. My stomach turned. Would I pass the nurse test?

Angela and I stood together in the hallway as the nurse worked her way down the line. "Stick out your tongue." She put a stick in Angela's mouth first.

I can stick out my tongue, I thought, and the pain in my stomach eased. The nurse put the depressor in my mouth and wrote something on a paper, then took what looked like chopsticks and parted my hair. She paused. "Kathy, go home and don't come back until you get rid of the bugs in your hair."

"Eeeeew." Angela scrunched closer to the wall. A ripple went down the line of kindergarteners.

"Next year," Gracie said to me after trying to get the bugs out of my hair. "We'll try again."

I never did get to cross Faile Street and stand in line with the kids who lived in my neighborhood, as the next year I was sent to Catholic school where my mother's former teacher at Cardinal Spellman was principal, and where tuition was waived for the Martin kids.

Instead of the warm classroom that smelled like wax where I dreamed I would learn everything, Catholic school brought the weight of Sister Joseph's ruler across my knuckles if I talked out of turn, or the shame of standing in the wastebasket if I forgot my homework.

It was a constant struggle to stay in school, and while I did graduate high school and find a job in Manhattan, life at home did not change. My mother continued to struggle to feed and shelter us, and when she wasn't working, locked the door to her bedroom where she could find a few hours of peace and quiet.

It was Brian who took me from that life of invisibility. It

was Brian who saw me in a way no one really had before. Clean shaven, civic-minded, a decorated veteran with a career in law enforcement before him, with Brian I wasn't a girl wearing hand-me-downs, I was a bomb squad officer's wife, a mother, a beautiful woman who was loved by a hero.

Nothing is permanent in this world,
not even our troubles.
— Charles Chaplain

The Funeral

THE MORNING OF THE FUNERAL BROUGHT THE MOST beautiful September weather I could remember, crystal clear skies, and a warm breeze. It was a day we should have been at the park, pushing Chris on the swings, spotting Keith on the monkey bars. The sun was a dirty trick lulling me into thinking everything was okay. I expected something to happen—the sky to explode in dangerous lighting—and longed to feel pounding rain.

Standing at the mirror, feeling thick from the tranquilizers doctors finally made me swallow at the hospital, I let my mother put yet another black dress over my head. We could hear the faint sounds of the media, could feel the pressure of them against the house. The polyester dress felt itchy.

"What about my good black suit?" There was a dress code at the office. We couldn't wear pants or skirts above the knee, and I thought the suit that cost more than I made in a week was perfect for a funeral.

"This is more appropriate," my mother said, and I didn't argue. It was hot out, and the dress did feel lighter than my suit, but when she tried to put a mantilla over my hair, I backed away.

"Are the boys coming?" Gracie stood in the doorway in an almost matching dress.

"They're with Amy across the street," my mother told her.

I was glad. I wanted the last memory of their father to be riding on his back, pulling a make-believe train whistle, not following his coffin out of St. Agnes Cathedral.

St. Agnes was where a bishop said mass on Sundays, and where Keith and Chris were baptized, though Brian preferred Father Donnelly from his Brooklyn parish, who would officiate the funeral mass. We lived on Long Island for five years, but Brian was a Brooklyn boy and would have been happy to stay in our first apartment, a brownstone on Beverley Road. I thought about how Brian helped me paint the bedroom chartreuse even though he said he didn't like the color, and how he laughed when I bought a sofa from one of the design centers we sold linen to without measuring the entrance to our apartment. We had to leave the sofa in the warehouse until we moved to Rockville Centre.

Now I wished I hadn't insisted we move into this house, wished that I spent more time with him instead of commuting into Manhattan to help pay for the home I now wanted to get away from. I wished a lot of things. That I didn't feel resentment when Brian went to the firehouse on weekends where he polished trucks and drank beer with other volunteers. I wished we made more time for each other. I wished for one more night. But it was too late for wishes.

Clinton Avenue was barricaded against the crowds. Out the limousine window, an ocean of blue uniforms and mourners, all silent, surrounded the Cathedral in the morning glare. The hook-and-ladder trucks from Brian's volunteer fire unit looked like giant toys glistening in the hot sun, piled high with flowers. His firemen friends stood awkwardly together, dressed in their blues. Rows of military uniforms lined up along the cathedral steps, men who had served with Brian in Vietnam. I closed my eyes. *This is all for you. They came to say goodbye.*

Every seat was taken. The St. Agnes Boys' Choir sang "Ave Maria," and Father Donnelly told the crowded church Brian died because of hatred and violence, a crime perpetrated by people who thought they could force the world to look at them. They called it a peace mission.

"But peace," Father Donnelly reminded us in his gentle, persistent voice, "cannot be gained by threatening, by blowing up an aircraft with over a hundred people on board, or by leaving a bomb in a New York City subway locker. The bomb that killed our beloved Brian Murray."

The sorrow of watching the bomb squad hoist up Brian's coffin blanketed me, and I wanted to die. I thought of the off-duty revolver I handed over to Charlie and wished I'd claimed I didn't know where it was. But then, who would raise our sons, who would carry on his memory?

"You are expected to follow," my mother whispered, and Paul and Bobby were there again, taking my arms, leading me down the aisle behind my brother Timmy and five bomb squad pallbearers.

Outside in the blaring sun, the old hearse with its curtained windows waited. But before they could load it, I felt myself reach forward. The crowds hushed, and I let my hand rest on the hot wood.

During the mile-long procession in the limousine, I saw neighbors line the sidewalks to watch Brian's body pass. The whole town of Rockville Centre seemed to be standing there. Traffic on Sunrise Highway was stopped. Police escorts stood at every street corner, and we passed the furniture store where we had just put a down payment on a dining room set, its purple and black mourning bunting bright in the sun. I laid my head back and stared at the tufted roof. It felt like I had left reality, the familiar, and crossed into what would become for me a dream-state where I allowed everyone else to make decisions—direct the future—because I couldn't see the future or even the next hour. I didn't even know where the cemetery was. We had been too young to talk about death. We weren't finished creating life. Just a week ago we'd decided to try for a daughter.

A thousand people were already at the gravesite. I sat in one of the folding chairs next to the coffin, my mother and Gracie on either side, the rest of my family and Brian's filling the rows. As we listened to the NYPD bagpipe band play a slow rendition of "Danny Boy," I remembered Brian and Tommy Monahan, his buddy from the Emerald Society, on lawn chairs in the yard, their cheeks puffed practicing the pipes for the St. Patrick's Day parade. Our kids and Tommy's two boys danced around, and laughed while Brian clowned and made his eyes bulge and his face turn purple.

An endless line of people placed flowers in front of the coffin. Finally, the Air Force fired a parting shot, a three-volley salute into the hushed crowd, and a formation of fighter jets left a plume of white cloud. One lone bugle player played taps. Then two decorated police officers removed the flag draped over Brian's coffin and began to fold it, each crease precise. When they put it in my hands, I stared down at the stitching on the white stars until it blurred.

AFTER THE FUNERAL I LAY in the dark bedroom again, leaving the boys to their grandmother. What would happen to them now? I thought about when we first had children, I kept my job so we could share parenting, a decision only partly based on economics. Brian wanted to help raise the boys, and we passed each other at three o'clock every day when I came home and Brian left for a four-to-twelve at the bomb squad. After growing up without a father of my own, I needed him to be their role model. But now, who would be there for them?

From the depths of sleep, voices drifted up from downstairs, and I heard Keith ask, "Are you a policeman like my daddy?" His voice floated up the stairs. *Who is he talking to?* I saw myself throw the covers back and shoot out of bed, my heart hammering in my ears, Keith's voice getting louder as I approached the stairs. A man's voice, deep, accented. "I'm not a policeman, but I know who your daddy was."

I flew down the steps in time to see his dark hair, his well-muscled back, and strong arms. He was headed for the kitchen, but by the time I got there he was out the back door. Keith looked into the dark after him.

"Who was that?" I asked him.

Keith shrugged. "He said his name was Zonko. He knows my daddy."

I woke from the dream with a start, soaked with sweat. *Zvonko Busic is in prison*, I told myself. *He can't hurt us.* But the vivid dream of that monster with my child would stay with me like a bad omen.

Fully awake now, downstairs I could hear my mother talking to Gracie. "Tell her to get up and take care of those kids." And then the front door opened and closed. I lay back in bed. That was the mother I remembered, not the one who held my hand on the way to the wake and the funeral.

Downstairs, the boys had discovered the refrigerator was filled with goodies neighbors brought over, and we played picnic in bed. Gracie kept them entertained when I was overcome again and again with a grief so stunning it rendered me speechless. The smallest thing could trigger my grief; seeing Brian's Criminal Justice textbooks still piled on his desk reminded me of his happy pronouncement, "I'll be done in December," and how when he'd said it I had mentally begun planning his graduation party.

When Gracie wasn't around, I let the boys watch cartoons and did my best not to cry. I tried to tame that restless rage that kept rising at will, tried not to think of those pictures in the bomb squad offices, photos taken after the FALN blew up Fraunces Tavern, killing four people, injuring fifty. Pieces of wooden chairs had been embedded in the victims' legs.

While Bugs Bunny chased the Road Runner, I thought about Father Donnelly's words, *a crime perpetrated by people who thought they could force the world to look at them.* What kind of people would do this?

The next morning I opened my eyes to the silhouette of my sister in the room. She was holding the tote bag I bought in Chinatown that I used during my commute. It usually held my high heels and whatever book I was reading. Now it looked like it was stuffed with clothes, and I wondered if she assumed I wouldn't need it anymore but didn't have the strength to ask. "I'm leaving. I have to go home." Outside the sun was shining. "I'll call you later."

I listened to her footsteps on the stairs. Heard her say something to the boys. I had been foolish to think Gracie would stay indefinitely. It wasn't her way. She was eighteen when she began to teach me how to leave. Boys were one way out, I knew, careers another, but when she stumbled through a haze of drugs at the threshold of her life, I made sure I found another door. Lying there with my own broken dreams spread out around me, I thought of Gracie's nearly fatal escape and her bloodstained bridal veil on the floor of our Faile Street tenement.

*He in his madness prays for storms
and dreams that storms will bring him peace.*
— Leo Tolstoy, *The Death of Ivan Ilych*

Broken Dreams

GRACIE PINNED HER HAIR IN A FRENCH TWIST AND STUCK in the last bobby pin before she walked from her bedroom out to the cellar to meet Jacky, who she called her James Dean. We all loved Jacky a little, with his blonde hair combed straight back, drowsy blue eyes, tight black pants, and white socks that peeked over wingtips.

"Here, kid." He smiled at me. "Buy yourself a Coke." Then he handed me a nickel. I looked out the window to watch them cross the yard, Jacky's arm around her shoulder, his head leaning in to listen to her soft words.

Gracie wore skirts that fell mid-calf, tight sweaters with matching neckerchiefs, and high heels that wobbled when she walked. She carried a black patent-leather handbag with a clasp that someone once twisted open while she was on the subway and then stole her wallet. Get a handbag with a zipper, my mother had warned, but Gracie was seventeen, worked at her first job as a receptionist at American Express, and was not about to carry an old lady's handbag.

"Kat," Gracie said when I picked up the phone one afternoon. "I left Jacky's ring on the bathroom sink. If you bring it to me, I'll buy you lunch."

I was nine-years-old, and, although I had taken the subway

by myself before, I had never been all the way downtown, or even past 42nd Street where my father worked, and now Jacky's ring was buying me an escape. "There's ten cents under the scarves in my top drawer. Take the #6 downtown from Hunts Point and get off at 125th Street. Cross over the platform for the #4 train to Wall Street. I'll meet you at the top of the stairs."

An hour later we were at Schrafft's sharing her favorite lunch. It was the late 50s, a time when ladies wore hats and gloves, and Schrafft's was a place a woman could dine alone amid the splendid architecture of the two-story restaurant and, if she was so included, sip gin from a teacup. It was where lovers could sit behind marble columns to hide from the public eye, and where, that day, the elegant interior made me feel like a princess.

I sat up tall and felt the excitement. *This is where I want to be,* I thought, as the bustle of Manhattan moved around me.

"What is Jacky going to do when you become a stewardess?" I asked Gracie.

American Express was temporary until she turned eighteen when she could apply for her dream job with an airline. She was still looking down at her hand, admiring the ring Jacky gave her when he graduated from high school.

"He'll get a job too." Gracie squeezed my hand. "What do you want to be?" She had never asked this question before, but I didn't need to think about it.

"I want to be a writer." I shrugged and smiled at the idea that had finally been put into words. Gracie nodded, watching me.

"What will you write about?" Her question was serious, not like she was talking to a kid. I took my time watching the blur of people moving toward important places.

"You."

DEAR DIARY: Gracie brought you home with her tonight. She said I could write about whatever I want and keep it

locked from our nosy little sister Annie. I'm going to keep
you with me all the time and write stories of Faile Street,
which I still hate, but now I'm used to living here.

"THREE MORE MONTHS UNTIL FLIGHT school." Gracie
made an X on the calendar she had nailed to the wall, the dates
crossed off until March 26, 1958, when she turned eighteen. "I
sent away for both applications, but I don't know which airline
I'm going to pick," she told me.

I knew it was between Pan Am and Eastern. Their posters
hung on the wall on either side of the calendar.

"Where will you fly?" I asked her, and although I had asked
this same question so many times, she thought for a minute as
she lit one of her Luckies and blew out the smoke in one cool
breeze.

"If I pick Eastern, I'll fly in the U.S. If I pick Pan Am, I can
fly everywhere."

The red-eagle Eastern airplane was headed for the sky, the
blue Pan Am globe promised the world. "Pan Am," I said. I
wanted the sun and the moon for Gracie. "So you can see the
world."

Out in the living room, I heard my mother say, "What are
you doing here, Tom?" My father still lurked around, even four
years after he had been kicked to the curb. "Get out," she yelled,
but a minute later, he was standing in the doorway to the room
Gracie now shared with me, an old storeroom with no heat that
she and Rose had painted pink and set up twin beds. Rose had
been gone two years, married and moved away from Faile Street
forever.

My father's face was dark with day-old whiskers, his suit
hung from his shoulders, and the flap of his shirt had come
untucked. He didn't love my mother or his children, but she was
still his wife, since he swore he would never give her a divorce. It
didn't matter that he had moved out and never showed concern
for any of us. It was the one aspect of his life where he still had

power, and in his eyes he was our father and what he said was sacrosanct. Sitting on Gracie's bed next to her, I could smell the Fleischmann's whiskey. He stepped into the room and squinted at the wall.

"Why are you crossing off dates?"

Gracie hesitated. She looked fragile, pale, her auburn hair swept back into a neat little dancer's bun.

His voice went up a notch. "I asked you a question."

"I'm counting down to my birthday," she said, her voice barely a whisper. "When I can go to flight school."

I inched closer to her, watching my father. There was something about his eyes, like a snake coiled, waiting to strike. "You're not going anywhere, young lady." He raised his chin. *Defy me,* it said, *and you will be sorry.*

"She's been dreaming about this for a long time, Tom. Let her have it." My mother's voice had lost the defiance she had gained in the years he was out of the house. She looked startled when he slammed her into the wall, her head striking the doorframe, knocking the wind out of her. She stood there like a child, holding the side of her head.

"She's not going to fly in any airplane." His twisted mouth exposed a dark space of missing teeth someone had knocked out years ago. He grabbed the calendar from the wall and ripped it in half. "Don't let me hear about flying again. Do you hear me?"

Gracie looked down at the torn pieces. "I hear you," she said softly. I felt stung by her surrender, sure I would have stood up for myself, would not have let my dreams be ruined by a father who had deserted us.

Gracie quit school at sixteen, as had Rose. It was something expected of us all, to bring home a paycheck. We weren't a family of dreamers, and maybe Gracie had known all along that her dream was as flimsy as a paper calendar, and that my father would dash out her dreams like you pinch out a budding rose before its blooming time. Gracie wasn't cunning. She had not known that to keep anything sacred in this family, you did not put it on the wall for everyone to see. Even locked in a closet, it could get stolen from you. My father, with his kicked-in teeth and hollow mouth, was a genius at broken dreams.

When he turned to leave, he found Corky standing in the doorway, blocking his way, a baseball bat in his hand. Corky's dark hair had grown from the short crew cut my mother insisted for the four boys, and now stood straight up on his head, untamed.

They stood eye-to-eye. My father's eye twitched first, acknowledging the strength of his fourteen-year-old son, and he stepped back.

DEAR DIARY: *Some day Corky will kill him and I'll be happy.*

GRACIE MARRIED JACKY JUST AFTER her eighteenth birthday. In his arms she felt safe from her father and safe from Faile Street, but in this single defiant act of marriage, I learned that you had to choose the right man for your escape, that choosing just anyone could leave you as imprisoned as the past from which you had tried to escape.

It was an hour before she would walk down the aisle, and already the ashtray on the dresser was filled with stubs of filter-less cigarettes. She tapped a Lucky Strike against her wrist, flicked a green plastic lighter until the cigarette caught, and then fidgeted with her hair, adjusting one last bobby pin before she lifted the pearl-studded bridal crown to her head. She looked like Cinderella. My mother stood at the doorway, her eyes brimming with tears.

"You can't wear pearls on your wedding day," she told her. "It's bad luck."

Gracie looked at her reflection in the mirror. "That's an old wives' tale, Mom. And anyway, Jacky's mother bought it, I can't disappoint her."

It was Annie, younger than I by twenty-one months, who

was the first to walk down the aisle in her pink ruffled dress, dropping rose petals, followed by Gracie holding my father's arm. He lifted her veil and kissed her cheek, then took a seat off by himself.

THAT NIGHT I LAY ON the sofa and reimagined Gracie dancing with Jacky, her dress gliding softly across the floor. I thought of the toasts to the new couple and cheers when they made their exit to begin their life together. But I woke to Gracie's shouts channeling through my groggy dreams. The sliver of light grew bigger as Gracie opened the cellar door, Jacky behind her, the pearl-studded crown off-center, the once-white shoes in her hand. Closing my eyes and I feigned sleep.

"You're high," Gracie said to her new husband. "I can tell you've been using, and I'm not going with you."

Jacky grabbed her. "You're coming, even if I have to drag you there, so get dressed." I stayed so still they didn't notice I was in the room.

"No," she twisted away, stumbling into the coffee table. I heard breaking glass, a soft cry. Gracie had cut her hand on the champagne glasses left over from the pre-wedding celebration, and I watched as scarlet blood dripped down the front of her Cinderella dress. We both jumped when Jacky slammed the door, rattling the windowpanes. Gracie looked at the blood as if it belonged to someone else.

"I'll get you a Band-Aid," I said as I jumped off the sofa.

A sob that had been building escaped and tears fell from her eyes. "Bastard."

The word wasn't meant for me, I knew, but my eyes welled up too. She walked out of the room. A few minutes later, she was out of the house, in the Rose Dirndl dress she bought for her honeymoon.

I looked around the room that my mother had spent the last of her energy cleaning and redecorating for the big day, the rug retrieved from lay-away already stained with champagne from the pre-party celebration. Lying on the floor next to the broken glass was the crown with the studded pearls, and the veil spotted with blood.

With Gracie gone and my mother working at the automat, just across town from the one where my father worked, I was in charge of the four little ones. Her job at the automat was a good one, my mother said, because she could bring home leftovers and there would almost always be something for dinner. Just like Gracie used to do, I gathered the little ones together on the couch and gave them a book to read. At eight, Annie could read pretty well, Timmy sounded out words, and Danny and Patrick took time out from destroying the apartment to listen to stories about the adventures of *Lassie* or *The Little Prince*. But when story time was over, there was little I could do to contain the cyclone that tore through the place. I missed my Gracie.

DEAR DIARY: *I had a dream last night that my mother told me a secret story, something, she said, that was between just the two of us. I want to write it down but her words were in Spanish.*

Gracie worked at the laundry folding towels until her baby came, and then one day she was home again. "What's the matter?" My mother watched Gracie pick up her Luckies and walk over to the stove where she took a wooden match from the box on the wall and struck it on the burner. It wasn't until she blew out the smoke that she answered. "Jacky's in jail."

Jacky would never meet his child, a boy Gracie named Matthew, blonde like him. He had stolen social security checks from mailboxes, forged signatures, and cashed them at the Southern Boulevard Check-Cashing store. He needed the money to buy drugs, and Gracie had looked the other way. He wouldn't change out of a prison uniform for twenty years.

DEAR DIARY: I will have Gracie all to myself again.

I WROTE IN THAT DIARY until the pages were filled and then used composition notebooks to write my stories. I wanted to share them with someone, but there was no one who cared, no oversight into what I was doing or what I needed, no one at home to follow up on homework or take an interest in my schoolwork. It was Gracie who had encouraged me, who had said I could do anything, who seemed the plausible solution to someone at home taking care that I made good grades. But after she moved back home she became distant, and without her to turn to, the world I lived in was limited, low ceilings, nothing to strive for, save being a waitress or a counter girl at the Horn & Hardart automat where my mother worked. There wasn't anyone to look up to who had gone to college or knew how to encourage high academic expectations. Taking books out of the library, I learned to write, but I wasn't a well-rounded student. I didn't understand math or science. I didn't get good grades. I never knew that I was smart or had any talent.

Around me the tide seemed to pull back and forth, pushing toward the unattainable as it had for Rose and Gracie and Corky, but I believed there must be a trapdoor, a secret hatch that could lead me into a world where opportunities existed, where the routes to freedom weren't blocked by a Faile Street address.

So it goes.
—Kurt Vonnegut, *Slaughterhouse Five*

Half Pay

BRIAN DELIVERED ME FROM THE PURGATORY THAT WAS Faile Street, but his death sent me to a level of hell from which there seemed no exile. It was a strange existence, living a life you were thrust into without choice or preparation. Floating in the ether of indecision, I kept surreptitiously turning to ask Brian's advice, picking up the phone to call him at work, searching for the portal back to the seven years we were happily married. While the city had come out for the wake and the funeral, after a few weeks, that fervor died down, and I felt completely and utterly alone with questions and no one to answer them.

I found it hard to get out of bed, to pour a bowl of cereal, to read bedtime stories to my sons. Depression wasn't really the word that captured how I felt. It was more like a complete shutdown; there was nothing left, no escape, no beauty, no sound that made a difference, not even the sound of my children's laughter. Outside, people came and went, took walks, laughed and cried, but none of that penetrated the darkness that covered my world. In the mirror, my face looked old and tired, my hair a neglected tangle. Brian often told me I didn't know how beautiful I was. Now, at twenty-eight, I didn't care, and beauty was the last thing on my mind.

I kept thinking about the irony of Brian asking for a transfer back into uniform right before he died, a painful decision for him since he loved the bomb squad and the team he worked with. He had been on the force six years, was considered an expert in his field, and dreamed of one day instituting innovative ways to more safely render devices harmless. Bomb disposal was the reason he went on the police force in the first place, and with his degree in Criminal Justice in sight, he saw himself moving up the ranks.

Only there were no promotions in the bomb squad because the unit had become part of the Technical Service Bureau, which was outside the purview of the Detective Bureau. While men like Paul and Bobby, who had come on the force with Brian, received their detective shields, the men on the bomb squad, who clearly worked as detectives, did not. This affected morale. They saw themselves left behind as others who had joined the force moved ahead, getting promotions and raises. He was tired of the excuses, and he wanted out.

I was the one who kept telling him to stay with the bomb squad, wait it out, that they couldn't withhold promotions forever. But the real reason I wanted him to stay was that statistics showed he had a better chance of being gunned down walking the streets of New York City in a blue uniform than being blown up by a bomb. The bomb squad had a stellar reputation for safety, with a single fatal explosion almost forty years before, compared with street cops whose names filled the walls of One Police Plaza. But now a bomb had exploded and plain clothes had not saved him. I needed to know why it happened, but the department had closed ranks, leaving me to grapple with the question alone. That familiar cloak of invisibility had descended again, and this time Brian wouldn't be there to lift it off me.

ON A MORNING WHEN MY mother came to Rockville Centre to take the boys to the playground, I finally managed to do my own grocery shopping, and when I came home, I found a sedan

I had never seen before sitting in front of our house.

"Kathleen Murray?" The driver ran to catch up with me when I got out of my car. "Bill Hutchinson." He offered his hand, but I didn't take it.

My arms were full of grocery bags. "If you're the press—"

"NYPD pension department." He cut me off and adjusted his thick, smudged glasses. I remembered vaguely someone was supposed to come by about my pension. The department had issued an initial insurance check, but there was still paperwork to be filled out.

"I'm scheduled to talk to you about your umm . . ." He looked out at the empty street. "Pension." He stood awkwardly, waiting for me to say something, not offering to help me with the bags.

He continued to fidget nervously once seated at my kitchen table while I put away the groceries and prepared coffee. *Why?* I wanted to scream at this nervous anxious little man. *Why did that bomb explode? Brian could dismantle a bomb with his eyes closed, why did this one explode and kill my husband?*

Instead, I asked, "Would you like anything in your coffee, Mr. Hutchinson?" I looked at the dandruff on his sloped shoulders and almost felt sorry for him.

"Black, please. Thank you." He was here before. I remembered now my mother coming up to the bedroom to tell me a Bill Hutchinson wanted to talk about my pension, but I told her to send him away. I thought his visit was simply a formality, the department would take care of us. I'd already told my boss to find a replacement. "The boys need me," I told Harry, and he agreed, said I could come back any time I wanted to, but I knew I wouldn't commute into the city again. I needed to stay home, close to my boys.

When I sat down Mr. Hutchinson opened his worn briefcase and spread his papers in front of me. "As of September 11, 1976, you will receive half of your husband's yearly salary. That amounts to $879.77 per month."

I stared at him. "Half?" He had the faint smell of old socks about him. "But I thought I would get three quarters. Don't injured officers receive three quarters?"

Bill Hutchinson smoothed his thin hair. "Yes, but, um, you see." His voice had a whining quality to it. "You have one less mouth to feed."

"One less mouth to feed? My sons just lost their father. How will I raise them on half of Brian's salary?" The way he looked at me made me want to scream with the awfulness of it all.

"Well anyway," he spoke quickly. "You will receive Social Security for yourself and your sons." He adjusted his glasses. "So that should make up for the loss in salary."

Did that mean I would have to leave my sons with a babysitter and return to work? I looked into his cloudy eyes for answers. "Is that how they reward their heroes?" I stared at his shiny, worn suit. "I don't even know what happened to my husband. Do you know how that feels? And now they are taking away half his salary."

Bill Hutchinson colored. There was a drop of spittle on the page he slid over for me to sign. "Again, we are sorry for your loss."

From the kitchen window, I watched him walk down our front path to his sedan. He walked on his toes as if perpetually about to fall on his face.

That night, when Gracie called, I told her that I had not been able to stop crying since he left. "He made it feel so final."

From the living room, I heard the commercial for Coca Cola, teaching my sons that if they drank soda, the world would be a better place. At four and two they already learned that they could not count on the world being better for them.

I looked around the pretty kitchen and saw Brian everywhere, the Formica counter tops he had replaced, the pantry he converted from a coat closet, his mug still sitting on the shelf. "What am I going to do in a month or two months or a year from now?" I asked Gracie. "I will still be alone with two boys to raise."

"Why don't you ask Mom to come stay with you."

I hesitated. I didn't like where the conversation was headed, and dried my eyes with a tissue. "She is staying with me."

"I mean permanently," Gracie said. "She can give you time to get back on your feet. It will give her a purpose."

"Is that why she has been so great?" I threw the bunch of balled up tissues in the trash. "Because she needs a purpose?"

"I don't know. Maybe it's because she realizes she missed her chance." Something in Gracie's voice sounded sad and distant, as though this were her life she was talking about as much as my mother's.

My mother had a heart attack a year before, but she had recovered nicely and was back to her job at Horn & Hardart. She talked about retiring, and moving in with the boys and me seemed to be the obvious solution. But I had to somehow move past my sorrow so I wouldn't miss my sons' childhood like my mother missed mine. I would ask my mother to move in, but first I had to figure out how to be there for the boys myself, how to make sure their lives were not hijacked as mine had been.

It might be that to surrender to happiness was to accept defeat, but it was a defeat better than many victories.
— W. Somerset Maugham, *Of Human Bondage*

Losing Gracie

As much as I loved Gracie, she had not been able to transform her pain and rage into action but had hidden from it behind the silky draw of a sweet high. And I spent my life trying desperately to choose another road. I knew for sure that Gracie and I were headed down different paths one Christmas long ago, and I had learned to make that hard choice on a snowy cold night on the streets of the Bronx.

My mother tried to keep out the South Bronx by installing four locks on the cellar door, but it was so warped it hung open like an invitation. That Christmas when I started to lose Gracie forever, she was standing, half-in and half-out of the cellar door, smiling at our attempt to get ready for Santa. Even with our coats on, we were freezing as we tried to string the lights.

I was all dressed up in my new outfit, a yellow dress with a flared skirt. Underneath, I was wearing a training bra, a garter belt, and silk stockings with a seam up the back just like my mother. Annie and I were meeting Angela and a few friends for midnight mass, and I wanted to show her off. She was eleven, and I envied her smooth blonde hair, un-freckled skin, and pouty lips. She looked beautiful, standing there holding the angel in her matching yellow dress and Maryjanes.

We had cleared the garbage cans and shovels out of the

corner so there was enough space for a tree, and Timmy climbed on the kitchen chair, took the angel from Annie, and balanced it on top.

Gracie stepped into the cellar and leaned against the cold cement, the dim overhead bulb gave her skin a gray cast. Recently she had been leaving her baby, Matthew, with Annie and heading out, we weren't sure where. Annie hated the fourth grade anyway and was happy to stay home and play mommy. I wondered if anyone else noticed Gracie slipping away. I felt it, the absence of the old Gracie who talked to me like there wasn't eight years between us, the Gracie who used to come home after a date with Jacky and tell me stories about dancing like Cinderella in a place so dark you couldn't see your hand in front of your face.

Now Jacky was serving twenty years for check forgery, and we weren't sure where Gracie was spending her time, except with her best friend Gloria, beautiful Gloria of the raven hair, cocoa skin, and charcoal half-moon eyebrows over shiny black eyes.

"Chu don' have shit to eat in dis house," I heard her tell Gracie. "Come to my house. I cook f'you."

When Gracie came home, sometimes days later, I asked questions with the innocent logic of a thirteen-year-old, "How come you look so sleepy?"

My mother's questions were harsher. "Where have you been? Why aren't you taking care of your baby?"

Gracie was in the apprentice stage then, gradually tiptoeing in on the lives of South Bronx junkies who lived in abandoned buildings and slept near radiators on cruddy mattresses.

"Where's Matthew?" Gracie asked.

"I just put him down for a nap," Annie told her.

"Here." I offered her a garland of lights. "Why don't you help us string some lights."

But Gracie didn't take the lights. "I can't stay." She ground her cigarette into the cement floor with the toe of her shoe. "I just want to see Matthew and then I have to meet George."

George, her new boyfriend from Long Island, drove a red Thunderbird convertible and sometimes let us pile into the back seat for a ride.

She went through the door that led to the apartment and came back with Matthew in her arms. He looked sleepy, slightly dazed. Gracie hugged him and kissed his face all over as he squirmed and finally started to cry, putting his arms out for Annie. But Gracie wouldn't let go. She fished her cigarettes out of her bag.

"Open the boxes." She lit up a Lucky Strike and took a deep drag. "I'll tell you where to hang the decorations." She looked sophisticated with the cigarette, and for a moment I saw the once-beautiful sister I loved like a mother.

At 6:30 p.m., the tree looking as Christmassy as we could manage, Timmy and I grabbed our coats and went to meet my mother at the train so we could help carry her shopping bags from the automat. Walking to the Hunt's Point train station, we played a guessing game about what we would have for dinner. Sometimes she brought dessert for dinner, bear claws she served with milk.

As soon as my mother emerged from the subway stairs I told her Gracie was at the house, and her eyes lit up.

"What'd you bring us?" Timmy asked.

"Mashed potatoes, chicken, baked beans, and," she smiled at me, "rice pudding."

Timmy and I looked at each other, excited about the feast, and hauled the heavy bags up Faile Street. At home we unpacked them in the kitchen.

"Where's Gracie?" my mother asked Annie, who was placing forks alongside each plate.

"She had to meet George, and took Matt with her."

"Oh Jesus." My mother put her hand on her chest. "She can't be out on Christmas Eve with that baby."

"She took the carriage and his blanket," Annie said, which made it okay with her.

"I don't care what she took with her. They're predicting six inches of snow tonight. Go find them."

"Maybe she's at Gloria's," I said hopefully.

"You know Gloria won't let George in. She hates him." My mother knew what I was too young to understand, that George, too, was a junkie looking for his next fix, and would drag Gracie down even further into the netherword of drugs. "Anyway, Gloria's probably with her family tonight. Go look around Kelly Street."

I was just about to protest when I saw tears brimming in her eyes, which brought home the gravity of Matt spending Christmas Eve in some tenement hallway.

On our way out we met Corky on the stairs. At seventeen, already a junkie himself, he would know better than me which drug den Gracie hung out in, but when I asked him if he could help us find Gracie, he said only, "I've got plans," and turned around to go back the way he came. No "Merry Christmas," no "I'll see you later."

"Merry Christmas. I hate you," I called after him.

As we walked along Faile Street, the cold wind went right through my coat. We passed windows decorated with spray-on snow and a manic-looking elf with glitter eyes that pranced toward the sidewalk. Lights twinkled on trees in the lobbies we passed, and, as we rounded the corner of Hoe Avenue, we could hear Bing Crosby's "I'll Be Home for Christmas" spilling onto the sidewalk. Curtains were opened in a ground-floor apartment, and I watched a family having dinner. Two parents and three kids. They looked cozy, and I thought for the hundredth time how nice it would be to have a small family. Row upon row of brightly-lit windows shuttered families inside, safe against the cold.

On Southern Boulevard, Wishner's Toy Store was still open. We watched a man wheel out a bicycle with a big red bow on it. Two women stood in line, toys piled in their arms. I knew the storeroom at home held boxes wrapped with Christmas paper my mother had hidden. They were from Aunt Delia, but my mother took off the tags to make it seem like they were from

Santa. I could peek inside the box with my name on it but loved the suspense almost better than the gift. I had asked for a girl's bike, again, and I liked to believe I might actually get one, just like the one the man in the store bought for his daughter.

"I'm starving," Annie whined. I had been saving a Hershey bar in my pocket and reluctantly broke it in half and offered her a piece of my coveted chocolate.

The moon was bright, the air cold enough to burn my nose. When the Westchester El roared by, we jumped back, not sure whether the flying white sparks would burn if they landed on us.

On Simpson Street, we held hands to brace ourselves against the wind coming around the Telephone Company Building. In winter, on our way home from school, it was often strong enough to blow us off the street. After a long block without any signs of life, we stopped at the corner. Looking up, I saw the street sign read Tiffany, not Kelly. "Where are we?" I could hear the fear in Annie's voice and realized we had gotten turned around.

My feet were screaming, the pointy shoes getting smaller with each step. Just as we were about to turn around and go back the way we came, three teenage girls stepped out of the shadows, tall as lampposts, like a tangle of black ghosts that sprang to life to scare the living shit out of us. Getting held at knifepoint or even gunpoint was an everyday event on these Fort Apache streets, and I felt myself step back.

I recognized one of the girls from school. Her name was Biffy, and she was big enough to swallow me whole. I stood still, waiting to see what she would do. I had been to her apartment in the Classon Point projects. Being invited to her place was a big deal and gave me a look at her poverty, which weighed even more than mine. Her bedroom had security gates that covered grime-coated windows. A broken mirror had been propped against a dresser, a bookshelf held rows of paperbacks, their bright jackets incongruous in that lifeless room. I had never gone back.

"Hey, how come you don't say hello," Biffy asked, pitching

her cigarette into the gutter.

"I'm sorry," I blurted out. "It's so dark I didn't see you."

Whoops and whistles came from her cohorts, and I realized my mistake. Biffy's skin was jet black. I was close to tears but laughed instead.

"You a funny girl." Biffy gave me a smirk. "You takin' your life in your own hands out here at night, but I'm a let you go cause it's Christmas."

"Thanks a lot," I said over my shoulder. "See ya." And then I grabbed Annie's hand and ran down the street, not caring that my shoes were rubbing blisters into my heels.

We double-backed, crossed over Simpson Street, and passed by the gated candy store where I often bought six-cent cokes. It was cold enough to scare the junkies off the street, scatter them to abandoned hallways where no one was celebrating Christmas. We stepped around flattened cardboard boxes and broken bottles. We checked the crashed-out tenements, Gracie's name echoing in the empty hallways when we called out to her. In one vestibule a group of young Hispanics gathered around a radiator. One of them stepped forward when I opened the door.

"I'm looking for Gracie or George. Have you seen them?"

"No, man. Ain't seen nobody," he slurred, so stoned I could have pushed him over.

A fire truck screamed by, momentarily diverting his attention, giving us the chance to get away. I opened another door to a wall of mailboxes gouged open. Scorch marks decorated the marble steps. I hated that Gracie frequented tenement buildings like these, where lobbies held the spoils of the lives of drug addicts, where the floors were littered with spoons and matches, so filthy and smelly you needed a gas mask to breathe. I had been to buildings like these before on other searches, and my best guess was that she could be found behind some dark stairway where no one could see her shoot heroin into her arm.

Close to 8:00 p.m., we stopped in front of the manger set up on the small lawn outside our church and studied the baby Jesus in his crèche scene. We had been looking for over an hour.

"Maybe if we go in and say about a hundred Hail Marys we'll find Gracie on the next street," Annie said half-heartedly.

There had been a time not so long ago when Annie believed flying reindeer would take her for rides over the rooftops of the Bronx. She didn't believe in much of anything anymore.

The church door opened, and out walked Angela with her mother, who had probably driven there in her car so Angela could set up flowers on the altar for mass. I wanted to hide, but they saw us.

"I thought we were going to meet up at my apartment before midnight mass." Angela didn't seem surprised to see us walking around. Helen, one of the few tenants my mother liked because she went to work and minded her own business, smiled at us.

"I know. I'm sorry. My mother sent us to look for Gracie, and we can't find her."

Helen's smile faded. "I can drive you home."

It was a treat when Helen drove us anywhere. No one in my family had a driver's license. Instead of accepting the ride and walking into our apartment without Matt, I lied.

"We'll be back in time for mass, I think I know where she is."

A few days before, Angela told me about the shopping trip to Bloomingdale's she took with her mother, and I noticed the proper coat and hat. I looked down at my own cheap, ruined shoes, and thought about Annie and me traipsing around the freezing streets on Christmas Eve, dressed all wrong. I hated her.

"All right." Her voice was light-hearted, like missing our night out was no big deal. "See you later." Helen looked back as they headed for their car, her arm around Angela's shoulder, her face now a worried frown.

"I'm freezing," Annie whined again.

And then I saw it: the green light outside the 41st Precinct. It was like a beacon that drew me forward. After more than an hour of wandering the streets, the light looked surreal.

"Let's go to the police."

"No!" Annie's expression was confused. "She'll get arrested."

"Listen to me," I said. "Matt is out there somewhere. He could be cold and hungry. It's not just about Gracie. She is probably stoned by now. She could forget about him and leave him in an abandoned building."

The wreath on the door of the precinct was a reminder of what we were missing out on tonight. Inside the warm reception area an officer sat behind a high wooden counter. He had black hair and a friendly face, and I made a weak attempt at a smile.

In a shaky voice I said, "Our sister is a drug addict who took her baby with her to get drugs. We've been looking for hours and can't find them. Can you help us?"

If Annie said the words they would have sounded more pathetic. I used her to ask for what I wanted when being cute was more important than being practical, but I could tell that the policeman took me seriously.

"Come with me." He was bigger than he looked behind the desk and had a twinkly smile he probably reserved for kids. He ushered us into a small room that smelled of stale cigarettes. "Sit here. I'll be right back."

We sat on the metal chairs, and he came back a few minutes later with two mugs of hot chocolate. His name tag read *Fallon*. "What's your name?" he asked.

"Kathleen, and this is Anne." She sat up straight, her hands folded in her lap like a good little girl.

"Where do you live?" Officer Fallon was tall, heavy-set with light brown eyes, and a mahogany voice. He was Paul Newman and Elvis Presley, and I fell a little bit in love.

"We live on Faile Street," I said, and Annie piped up, "It's not like she kidnapped her son or anything." Annie was irresistible, and I could tell he thought so too.

"We've been up and down Faile Street, Southern Boulevard, Hoe Avenue, and even Tiffany Street." My senses felt heightened, intrusive, my new bra and garter belt rough and scratchy. The taste of hot chocolate lingered on my tongue, sweet and gummy. "We wanted to go over to Kelly Street, but were turned around." The 41st Precinct was in the worst neighborhood in the Bronx, and Kelly Street was off the radar. You did not want to walk around there, especially in the dark.

Officer Fallon looked like a family man, the kind of father I wanted all my life, and I watched him while he wrote down our words.

"Do you have any kids, Officer Fallon?" I asked.

"Two sons." He brightened a bit, and his smile seemed out of place in the room. "Five and seven."

"I guess they're waiting for you to come home for Christmas." He would own a car, I imagined, and drive home to a tree-lined street lit with holiday lights.

"We'll have Christmas tomorrow. Someone's gotta work Christmas Eve, and I won the privilege. By the way, call me Officer Tom. My father is Officer Fallon."

I thought about Officer Tom's two boys and how they must love roughhousing with their father, how excited they must be anticipating his coming home. I pictured his wife as she looked into his soft brown eyes and said, *I love you*. I pictured his living room filled with great gifts and the boys tearing open all their dreams come true.

"Stay here. I'll try to find your sister and her son and be back before you know it."

The room felt empty when he shut the door, and we sat in the small, dirty space that was once painted green and was now a sooty-gray, the only furniture the scarred table and four metal chairs. There were no windows, and the bright bulb in the ceiling put a sharp edge on everything.

We sat quietly, warming our hands on the hot cups. My feet were freezing and on fire at the same time; I released them from the crippling shoes and wiggled my toes. When I looked down, they were red and swollen, my nylon stockings pooled around my ankles.

I should have been a stranger in that precinct, but the truth was I had been there many times, when my father beat up my mother, when Corky beat me up. That was the short list. I watched Annie swing her Maryjanes back and forth, the ruffle of her white socks blurring. Her hair, which we took so much time to fix, now looked like it had not been combed at all. She was still beautiful, her cheeks rosy, her pouty lips red from the cold. She was missing her first midnight mass, the first time she was allowed to stay up on Christmas Eve, but she had not said a word about it.

"What do you think we'll get for Christmas?" I asked her.

"I don't know." She was just past the Santa stage. "Not a doll, I hope." She rubbed her arms. Her coat was too thin, not really suited for a cold winter night like this. She had picked it out when Delaney, our mother's cousin, brought us to Alexander's for our Christmas gift, thinking the red color Christmassy, excited when she bought it, never imagining she would wear it to find her sister on freezing streets.

The hot chocolate made me feel warm and sleepy, and I considered putting my head on the table, but the door opened and I saw the wobbly wheels of Matt's carriage. Officer Tom ushered Gracie in. It had only been a few hours since I last saw her, but already her hair looked oily, her clothes grimy.

"Found them on Kelly Street, just like you thought." He nodded to me. "She and her boyfriend were sleeping in a hallway." He shook his head at her like he was disappointed. "Her boyfriend is in lockup. The baby seems fine." Both Annie and I peeked into the carriage where Matt looked warm and cozy.

"When did he eat last?" Annie asked.

"He had a bottle about an hour ago. I took him to Gloria's where I fed and changed him." Gracie gave her a long look. "I *am* his mother."

I saw Annie's eyebrows shoot up, like this was debatable. I watched Officer Tom fill out paperwork and wondered what he would do with Gracie. I was too afraid to ask.

"Let's go." He stood up. "I'm going to walk you home," he said. "I'd like to talk to your mother."

Matt was still sleeping peacefully, unaware of his surroundings, and we strolled down Southern Boulevard as snowflakes began to swirl softly from the sky.

"Can I get a cup of coffee?" Gracie asked when we passed the Boulevard Diner.

"Sure," Officer Tom said.

Inside the empty restaurant, we sat in one of the red leather booths and parked the carriage next to us. A waitress came over, and without asking, Officer Tom ordered apple pie à la mode for everybody.

"I'm not hungry." Gracie gave a weak smile to the lady. "Just coffee, thanks."

I watched her pour half the sugar-jar into her coffee cup. She couldn't stop moving, twitching, scratching, wiping her nose. *Please, just leave me here and go home without me*, her eyes pleaded. But I couldn't leave her. A police officer was sitting with us and there was no going back. I looked out the window of the coffee shop into the ruined night and said a prayer for my sister. *Please, God, just let her kick drugs and make her back into the old Gracie.*

Outside, a light coating of snow had settled on the deserted streets, showing the track marks of Matt's coach carriage. Officer Tom helped us down the cement stairs with the carriage and walked through the dark passageway where someone had broken the light bulb again. My mother was waiting for us in the kitchen.

"Thank God." Tears were streaming down her face. She looked like a shadow of my mother, smaller, less imposing. The overhead pipes were unusually quiet, and the radio was playing "Jingle Bells" softly in the next room. The little ones were asleep, and my mother had been sitting alone on Christmas Eve for hours, a cup of cold coffee with a smudge of lipstick on the rim, an overflowing ashtray in front of her. A few moments passed before she saw the police officer, and I caught the hesitation, the relief that everyone was all right usurped by the fear that a cop was standing in her kitchen.

Annie reached into the baby carriage and picked up Matt,

holding him to her. She looked too small to be holding a baby, too young, but she was the one who knew what should be done. "I'm going to put you to bed," she told him.

I went to the bathroom to wash off the stink of the Bronx streets, and when I came out, Gracie was sitting on the living room couch alone, watching the blinking lights from a strand of fake garland my mother had strung over the doorway. The air in the room felt heavy and even the blinking lights seemed to have slowed, as if the spirit had gone out of them. She was still wearing the same pilled red sweater and black pants with the hem coming down. Her worn-out shoes had been tossed aside, and a bone-like knuckle stuck out of her red, chafed feet. I made a mental note to give her my gym sneakers and some warm socks, but I didn't get up. Taking off my shoes, I rubbed the circulation back into my toes, and ran my hand over the blisters. Gracie studied the nails she had bitten down to nubs. She was 21 years old and looked 40.

"He found drugs." She glanced up at me. "They arrested George." She didn't ask me why I had gone to the police. She seemed resigned to her fate.

I squeezed my eyes shut trying to drown out the clamor she unleashed in my mind. When I opened them, I could tell she was thinking it over to see what kind of new pattern jail would make in her life. I started to say something reassuring but let it go. She was too preoccupied to listen, her blue eyes glazed over. I could smell the fear on her, the disease.

Finally, she lit a cigarette and watched the fire burn down the match until it was a little black stick, then tossed it in the ashtray. When she looked at me I saw a plea. Years of sisterhood made us able to communicate without words. She wanted me to help her tame whatever demons had ahold of her. But there were so few options for me, a thirteen-year-old girl in the base-ment of a Bronx tenement.

We listened as our mother sat in the kitchen pleading for Gracie's freedom. In the end, Gracie was allowed to go live with Aunt Delia to detox and get clean. "I'll kick the habit,"

Gracie said, standing next to Officer Tom in our little kitchen. "I promise." But somewhere in me, I knew I had lost my sister. I had picked law and order over her, and things would never quite be the same between us after that. And though Gracie would continue to leave and come back into my life, I understood that I would have to make a choice for a different kind of sisterhood if I didn't want to end up like her.

Everything we hear is an opinion, not a fact.
Everything we see is a perspective, not the truth.
— Marcus Aurelius

Behind the Shield

"COME ON, GET UP," PAUL YELLED UP THE STAIRS A FEW days after Mr. Hutchinson brought news that I would receive half Brian's salary. "I'm on loan from the department for the week." Paul was one of the few NYPD who kept in touch. He and Brian had been close friends since their days at the academy. Paul and Roseanne were Chris's godparents. "I plan to take my role in his life seriously," he said right after the funeral. "I want to be there for him and for Keith."

"Shush," I called down, trying to find my robe. *How did he get in?* "The boys are sleeping."

"No they're not," Paul called back. "Keith let me in. They're in the kitchen having breakfast."

I never heard them. These days, I was either awake all night or slept like the dead. In the kitchen, I stepped on cereal covering the floor. Paul was working on a pile of dishes still in the sink.

I ruffled Keith's hair. "Chris." I looked at my little boy who needed a bath. "You know you're not supposed to get out of your crib." An acrobat, Chris could do flips out of his crib with one hand. A few weeks ago, my neighbor called to tell me he was standing on the second-floor windowsill.

"I climb out," he said.

81

"From now on call Mommy when you want to get out, okay?"

He played with his cereal while I kissed his head.

"What do you need me to do today?" Paul put a cup of coffee in my hands.

"I would like to see Terry McTigue." Except for the market, I had not been out of the house in three weeks since the funeral. "Would you drive me to Jacobi Hospital?"

Paul was quiet. Jacobi Hospital in the Bronx was where they took Brian after the explosion and where he died. I watched him put a plate in the dishwasher.

"Sure," he finally said. "Roseanne would be happy to take the boys." He found the soap under the sink. "But don't you want to give it a little more time?"

"I want to talk to him." Terry McTigue ran the bomb squad. I didn't know him well, but I had met him a few times. He was still alive, and the least he could do was talk to me. He would know what happened to Brian and why that bomb exploded.

"Okay," Paul said, but he didn't look at me.

As we drove to his house, I saw the strain of losing his friend had been etched in Paul's face, and I longed to see the old Paul again, the one whose eyes misted with tears of joy when Roseanne told me I was pregnant with Chris after I had missed the clues. It seemed like yesterday the four of us went to see *The Godfather* and had four different opinions about the movie. We had two boys, who often played with their two girls. The idea was they would grow up together, be best friends.

When we pulled up in front of their house Roseanne was waiting, and she crushed me in a bear hug that knocked the air out of me. I could smell the hairspray in her lacquered bouffant. It reminded me of the day a few years ago when two cops were gunned down, and I had driven over to her house so we could be together, two police wives crying over the loss of a young cop and the possibility one of us could be next. Now that it was my husband, I wasn't sure I could pretend our friendship was the same. She still had her husband.

While the boys dodged around to get big wheels from her garage, Roseanne rocked me back and forth. "I'm going to cook dinner for you." She leaned back and looked at me, snapping her gum with her super white teeth. "Some of my famous home-made pasta." It was a statement. You couldn't say no to Rose-anne.

Paul picked up Suzanne, a few months younger than Chris. Watching him, I wondered for the hundredth time how the boys would fare without Brian, what mark they would make on the world with me as their sole parent. Keith was bright, startling me at four years old with his ability to read and his penchant for books. And Chris was a child unafraid of danger, athletic and agile at two, quick to answer math problems.

Back in Paul's car I held onto the door handle. The hot metal stung my palm, but somehow it felt good, and as we crossed the Throgg's Neck Bridge, I looked down at the turning water and had the odd thought I might just open the door and fall out.

He kept the car windows open and Elton John and Kiki Dee were singing "Don't Go Breaking My Heart" on his radio. The song made me think about Brian singing those words, his hand over his heart, so I would take pity on him after he made me late for work, and I held tight to the burning metal.

When we passed Pelham Bay Park I tried not to look, and thought about how I could never escape the Bronx. Helicopters and police boats were housed at Rodman's Neck, the world's largest machine shop for weapon development, the NYPD firing range, and riot control equipment. It also held the pit, where the bomb squad destroyed unexploded devices. This pit was where the bomb truck had gone after it left Grand Central the night of the hijacking. During a detonation, the men could climb out of the pit and take cover behind a wall of sandbags.

My thoughts turned to Terry McTigue and what he might be able to tell me. I knew he sustained serious injuries from the bomb blast, but I hoped he would be able to talk to me. Although Inspector Behr commanded the Technical Services

Bureau, he was more a figurehead; it was Terry who ran the bomb squad. Officially he was a sergeant, but realistically he was the boss, the most decorated, and one of the world's foremost bomb technicians. Brian had admired Terry, talked about him all the time, how brilliant a technician he was, how lucky he was to be under his command. The whole squad thought so. They were a tight bunch, depending on each other for their lives. If one man made a mistake, he could blow them all up.

"You all right?" Paul asked.

"I'm okay," I told him. I looked out at Pelham Bay Park at a little boy roller-skating with a red balloon. I had played in that park as a little girl, made sand castles on that beach. Brian and I had married in a church just a few miles away. Now I couldn't stand to look at it.

A police officer was standing in front of McTigue's room when we walked down the hallway, and Paul showed him his badge. The door was open, but the officer didn't move.

"We're here to see Terry," Paul said.

I could see past him to McTigue, lying in bed. He seemed to be asleep, his bandaged head lopsided. A chain suspended from the ceiling held up his wrapped hand.

McTigue opened one eye, the other was hidden under the bandage. He looked right at me but didn't seem to recognize me. I tried to walk in, but the officer blocked my way. "Wait outside please." He turned, went into the room and said a few words to McTigue. When he came out again, he closed the door behind him. "Sergeant McTigue does not wish to see you."

"But did you tell him who it was?" I asked. "I'm Kathleen Murray."

"I know who you are, Mrs. Murray." The officer looked at the wall behind me. "And I am very sorry for your loss, but Sergeant McTigue does not wish to see you."

I watched his mouth twitch slightly and felt myself go cold.

"Mrs. Murray would just like a minute with him," Paul said.

The police officer was still looking straight ahead. "Sergeant McTigue does not wish to see her."

"I don't understand." I looked up at Paul. "Why won't he see me?"

"This was a mistake." Paul put his arm around me. "You're not ready for this. Let me take you back home."

But I couldn't just walk away, not when I was so close to talking to the one person who could tell me the truth about how the bomb exploded, how Brian died.

"If I write a note," I asked the police officer, "would you give it to him?"

He nodded slightly.

At the nurse's station, I scribbled on a pad of paper the RN slid over, writing about my concern for him, how I wished him well. Then I handed it to the officer, and we waited outside the closed door while he went in to deliver it. The officer came back out and shook his head.

"What did he say?" I asked.

"I'm sorry, Mrs. Murray. He does not want you to come back."

"Why?" I kept asking Paul on the ride home. "I don't understand."

"I don't know." Paul shook his head. "Usually when there's a line of duty death everyone tries to help out the widow."

As we were going back over the Throgg's Neck Bridge, it dawned on me: Not one member of the bomb squad, except for Charlie, had called me since the funeral. In the days after Brian's death, the department had been a constant presence, except for the men on the bomb squad, who had been like brothers to him. Why weren't they talking?

At dinner, I pushed the food around on my plate.

"Eat more, honey." Roseanne was already finished and smoking an after-dinner cigarette. "You need more meat on those bones."

"Come on," Paul said finally. "I'll take you home."

"BOMB SQUAD," JERRY KELLEHER SAID later that evening

when he answered the phone.

"It's Kathleen Murray," I squeezed the phone in my hand. "I just wanted to know if you have any information for me about how Brian died." Jerry managed the office, and was one of the oldest members of the bomb squad. He had rotated jobs with Brian. "Any more specifics?"

"Not yet," he stammered. "Do you want to talk to Charlie?" He couldn't hand the phone over fast enough.

There was a time when I joked with Jerry, asked about his kids, a time when he told me stories about the antics of Brian and Charlie, the youngest men on the squad, who shot blank bullets into the forensic water tank to see who could get off the most shots in a minute, or set a trash-can fire to see how long it would take to fill the room with smoke. Scientific research, Brian said with a smile when I asked if he had gotten into trouble.

Jerry had sided with Brian on what station to play on the old FM radio, so that it was big band music, Dizzy Gillespie or Gene Krupa, that played in the background when I called. And he named Brian best dressed. They worked in plain clothes, and Brian wore plaid jackets with wide lapels and ties, slacks that flared over spit-shined shoes, his hair combed carefully across his brow, sideburns slightly curved toward his lips, auburn mustache. He coordinated every outfit, his closet militarily ordered, complete with a shoeshine box left over from his Air Force days.

"Can you come over tonight?" I asked Charlie when he came on the line. "I need to talk to you."

"How's eight?"

"Do you have any information about the hijacking?"

"I saved it all for you," he said quietly.

I had two hours to wait. Keith and Chris ran around, taking out one toy after another while I became more convinced something was very wrong, something the bomb squad and the department were keeping from me. My nerves were on fire.

I sat Chris on my lap to keep him from running through

the house. He was approaching his third birthday. Too young to understand, his sometimes hopeful voice asked, "will Daddy come home today?" Brian and I often discussed what a tough kid Chris was, and marveled that he could get back up after a fall without a tear, jump into the cold ocean, run barefoot on hot sand. I was afraid he would grow into a young man so strong that I would not be able to hold him down. I hugged him against me to keep him still, to hear his little heart beat.

In contrast, Keith was a quiet child, pensive and already doubtful. I watched him fit together magnet letters on his slate: stop, no, sno. The other day he insisted on new underwear without cartoons. Daddy pants, he said.

When he was nine months old, I left Keith playing on the living room rug while I went to the bathroom. Somehow he managed the screen door, crawled down the three steps, and was halfway to the curb by the time I noticed his absence. When I scooped him up he looked at me with eyes that seemed too wise, as though he knew where he was going and how he was going to get there, and I had spoiled his plan.

"I'll read you a book," I finally told the boys. "And then it's bedtime, okay?"

In the last weeks, they slept with me most nights, and I loved their warmth, loved listening to their breathing, watching them sleep. But tonight I needed to be alone. I had to think. We sat on Keith's bed and read *Swimmy*, and, even though it was still light outside, I tucked them in. Chris began to cry. "I want to sleep in Daddy's bed."

"Me too," Keith told me. "I'm scared to sleep in here."

Daddy's bed. Something they needed as much as I did. "Okay, but only if you go right to sleep."

"We will," they both said in solemn voices. They were so good, their voices low, their arguments settled without coming to me.

I looked at my little boys side by side in our bed as they began to doze off and thought about Brian when he was a little boy. It was likely his mom didn't sit on the side of his bed until he fell asleep. She had died from liver failure three years after we were married, but he told me about her, how she spent most of her time in bed, drunk, how he wanted to give his boys something far different than that.

"And we will," he told me, kissing my forehead.

Downstairs, I watched out the window for Charlie's car and kept thinking about that morning I opened the door to find him on our porch. *I have to get out of here,* I thought. *Move away.* Start a new life where not every single thing was a reminder of the life I no longer had.

Finally, because the waiting was torture, I walked to the liquor cabinet we had inherited from Brian's parents, took out a bottle of scotch, and poured some into one of the fancy glasses we never used. I had not had a Dewar's in years, and it tasted awful, but felt good going down, so I poured another one and sat on the couch to wait. I wished Gracie were here, her soothing voice telling me I was strong, that I could face anything, but Gracie had her own life, and the hollow space she left behind only made me miss Brian even more.

"Would you like a drink?" I asked when Charlie came through the door. Wearing brown low-rise bell bottoms and a sweater vest, he reminded me of Ted Baxter on the Mary Tyler Moore show.

He was carrying two boxes. "No thanks." He set them on the floor. "You go ahead." I watched him settle into the brown velour chair across from me, where Brian used to sit.

"I heard you went to the hospital to see McTigue." He drummed his fingers on the armrest.

"I thought he would tell me what happened." I sounded pathetic, even to myself.

"He won't talk to you." Charlie looked down at the boxes. "Had you asked, I could have saved you the trip." He sounded sarcastic, biting. *Had you asked.*

I stared at the amber liquid and thought, *if I drink enough of this I won't feel anything.* "Who will talk to me, Charlie?"

I expected some platitude: they are just giving you time, or they don't want to intrude. Instead, an awkward silence ensued. The silence didn't feel like Charlie. It felt more like I was sitting across from a strange authority from whom I desperately needed something.

Finally, I asked the question that had kept me awake nights. "Was the bomb booby-trapped?"

"It didn't seem to be." Again, a vague answer. They would have known the first day, when they examined every grain of sand at the explosion site.

We waited together in the living room that had become part of the nightmare. It was somehow still filled with ghosts of the NYPD who stood in stiff uniforms with gold braids, here to inform the widow.

Charlie didn't try to fill in the uncomfortable silence with small talk, and he wasn't going to volunteer any information either. This wasn't the Charlie who made working at the bomb squad an adventure for Brian. That Charlie was funny, livened up the tedium of waiting for a call with pranks that kept the squad on their toes. This also wasn't the Charlie whose little girls walked on their daddy's shoes, climbed on his back, and plastered stickers to his forehead.

A few minutes passed before I got up the nerve and voiced my deepest fear, the one I had not been able to speak aloud.

"Was it Brian's fault?" I felt so dizzy after I said it that I had to focus on a spot on the carpet to make sure I didn't pass out. Or throw up.

"No." Charlie's voice was steady, sure. "Brian was standing back, to the left of the device. We don't know how the bomb exploded." He emphasized each word as though he were trying to make me trust them.

I tried to let his answer settle without it turning into a sharp-edged sword that threatened to cut me open. I couldn't believe they didn't know. It was their job to know, to fit together the pieces and come to a determination. It was what Brian loved about the job, coming up with evidence. I thought about asking whether McTigue was responsible, if he thought it was obvious because McTigue's fingers had been blown off, but an accusation like that would surely alienate me from the only person on the bomb squad who would talk to me.

Instead, I asked, "Why don't you have bomb suits?"

He didn't seem surprised. This was something Brian had complained about, that other, less prestigious departments had better equipment than the City of New York.

"The suits aren't required equipment."

That dizzy feeling came back. "Could a bomb suit have saved Brian's life?"

"They're still in the development stage. We're looking into them." I waited before asking my next question to let him continue to steer, and watched to see where he would go, but he stopped talking and let the air hang with his clipped words. The silence itself spoke volumes.

"What do I do now, Charlie?" My words were more forceful then I intended. "How do I tell my sons the bomb squad doesn't know how the bomb exploded that killed their father, or why he wasn't given protective gear?" I looked at him hoping he would remember what Brian meant to him, what his answers meant to me now.

Charlie rose. I watched him go into the kitchen. He knew his way around, and I heard him brewing coffee. When he came back, he was holding two steaming cups.

I took one of them. "I need to know what happened."

Charlie sat back down. "There's no way to find out." He sipped his coffee. And then, almost as an afterthought, he said. "Unless you sue the department."

"Sue the police department? Make an enemy of the NYPD?" The idea of it made me feel all shivery inside.

"It's probably the only way you'll find out exactly what happened," Charlie said.

I looked at the neatly stacked boxes of files and newspapers on the floor. *Hijacked!* The top headline read. "If McTigue would just tell me what happened, I won't take this any further."

Charlie shook his head. "No one will talk to you." His words were so cold they frightened me. He picked up the boxes and walked over to the dining room table where he began unpacking newspapers and then files with the navy and gold NYPD patch. He seemed to have a system, and I let him organize them across the table. "I'll leave these for you to read when you want to."

News of the hijacking had taken up the front pages of every major newspaper in the nation, but it would be usurped by the Supreme Court ruling for the death penalty, the election of a peanut farmer, and Jack Nicholson in *One Flew Over the Cuckoo's Nest*.

"Can I ask you something?"

Charlie looked at me. "Sure."

"Did Brian know he was going to die?"

The blood seemed to drain from his face, and he stood still for a few seconds. Charlie was a marine and had seen combat in Vietnam. I was sure he knew the answer.

"No." I saw him swallow. "He didn't know what hit him. When dynamite explodes there's no delay, there's no time to think. It's immediate. Nano-seconds."

I looked behind him at the newspapers spread across the table and gripped the warm coffee to steady myself.

"What did he look like?" I was sorry I asked the minute I spoke the words, but I had thought about it, imagined it when I saw the closed coffin, and I had to know.

Charlie put his hand on a stack of newspapers as though to protect them from a strong wind. He didn't look at me.

"By the time I got there, he was on the way to the hospital. I never got to see him. Jerry Kelleher stayed with him." He straightened an already straight file. "Brian looked just like he always looked. A piece of metal caught him in the throat. That's how he died."

I didn't believe him. *Unsuitable for viewing*, went skittering across my mind, the words Paul had said at the funeral. My brother Timmy had identified Brian's body and wouldn't answer me when I asked the same question. I could have challenged Charlie. But I held on to the picture in my head, the one my mother had given me at the wake, the one with Brian wearing his blue uniform and his wedding ring.

After I heard Charlie's car door slam, I took a copy of *The New York Times* from the top of a neat pile. Photos of Brian and Terry and Hank were lined across the front page. Below their photos was the Croatian: Zvonko Busic, raising his hands in protest. His dark, unruly hair and full beard made his face look wolfish, menacing. Beside him was his wife. I let my eyes rest on her long hair, her knee-length skirt, that slight, thin-lipped smile. "Julie Busic," the caption read. "Wife of the Terrorist." I scanned the article and found it horrifying how our lives paralleled one another. We had been born the same year, met and married around the same time, and for a few years, we even worked a few miles apart in Manhattan. She was blonde, fair, slender. She didn't look like a hijacker. I studied her face in the newspaper, and longed to change the truth, curve the details so it was she who had lost the man she loved, not me.

*There is a sense in which we are all
each other's consequences.*
— Wallace Stegner, *All The Little Live Things*

The Crime

THE MORNING AFTER CHARLIE'S VISIT I WOKE TO SUN streaming through the window, and it took me a moment to remember. For a split second I felt I had been transported back in time, when I was able to look over at Brian sleeping, listen to him breathe, and in his absence there was a moment of inexplicable panic, as if Brian were a little boy and I had lost him in a crowd. Now it still shocked me to see his wallet missing from the night table. I rolled over and kissed Chris's damp forehead, then Keith's.

"Wake up sleepy heads."

As the boys ate their cereal, I stared out the window where Chris's big wheel sat in grass overgrown in the weeks since Brian had cut it. The boys complained that my peanut butter and jelly sandwiches weren't the same, a trip to the park with me not as much fun. Keith called for Daddy when he fell down or when I said "no." He woke screaming at night, and I sat in the dark trying to soothe him, reassure him I was never going away. But it was Daddy he wanted.

I took a sip of cold coffee and rubbed my temples against a headache that seemed always to be waiting for me. The fan belt had come loose on the old Chevy, soon there would be snow to shovel, the bathroom faucet had dripped a blue stain on the sink. My mother was tying up loose ends in the Bronx, and I had made room for her in Brian's study where she would sleep on the pullout sofa, but somehow the arrangement didn't feel right. Her coming felt complicated instead of comforting, dredging up old memories I thought I had left long behind me when I married Brian. Did I really want my mother in my life every day?

In Brian's study, the e.e. cummings poetry book he had been assigned for English class still sat on his desk. I read the books he brought home for class during my half hour commute from Rockville Centre to Penn Station, and this thin volume held a poem that for some reason I read many times.

and what I want to know is
how do you like your blue-eyed boy
Mister Death

As I recalled the lines, a shiver went down my spine, and I grabbed a yellow pad and a pen and quietly closed the door to the room Brian once claimed as his sanctuary. Before falling asleep the night before, I had devised a note-taking strategy for the papers Charlie brought over, mentally dividing the topics of Hijacking, Explosion, and Hijackers. Sitting at the dining room table, I began piecing together what happened from the various reports and myriad media.

On September 9th, 1976, the night before the planned hijacking, the Busics had dinner at the top of the Gulf and Western Building on 59th and Broadway to go over the plan. While they enjoyed their last night of freedom, Brian and I fell asleep together, still believing in the possibilities of our lives.

While the Busics took a taxi to Grand Central Station, carrying a heavy shopping bag filled with explosives, Brian prepared to take his sons to the park. He loaded their bikes into the trunk and packed a bag with drink boxes and pretzels. When the Busics sought out the perfect locker space, one big enough to hold the cast iron pressure cooker, I was at my desk, a five-minute walk across town, unaware of the couple standing in the station concourse, unnoticed by hundreds of travelers, holding a bomb that could kill everyone and demolish the century-old landmark.

After putting the bomb in the locker, they took a subway to La Guardia Airport, arriving at the end of a security shift to avoid scrutiny. No one paid attention as they walked through security separately, each holding pieces of what would turn out to be fake devices, a duplicate of the real one they left in the subway locker. No one noticed their suitcases were filled with leaflets.

At 7:30 p.m. on Tuesday, September 10th, they boarded Trans World Airlines Flight 355 headed to Tucson, with a stop-over in Chicago.

When the plane took off, a few of the eighty-six passengers aboard noticed, but made no comment, when Busic, a raffish-looking man with a black beard, made several trips to the lavatory. There, he filled empty cylinders with silly putty and wrapped them with duct tape he carried on board. Dr. Richard Brockman, a passenger, took notes during the flight and the pages read that there was a blonde girl about twenty-five who kept going back to the restrooms. She had a good figure. She seemed anxious, in a hurry.

Ninety-five minutes into the flight, Busic emerged from the toilet with wires around his neck, black tape holding the mock dynamite in place. Entering the cockpit, then accessible to passengers, he handed the pilot a note. Captain Richard Carey had been trained to remain calm and cooperate with hijackers, and he read the note quietly as the plane moved through the air.

The note said:

1. This airplane is hijacked.

2. We are in possession of five gelignite bombs.

3. We have left the same type of bomb in a

locker across from the Commodore Hotel on 42nd
Street. To find the locker take the subway
entrance by the Bowery Savings Bank. After
passing through the token booth there are three
windows belonging to the bank. To the left of
these windows are the lockers. The number of the
locker is 5713.

4. Further instructions are contained in a
letter inside this locker. The bomb can only be
activated by pressing the switch to which it is
attached, but caution is suggested.

5. The appropriate authorities should be noti-
fied immediately.

6. The plane will ultimately be heading in the
direction of Paris, France.

Dr. Brockman, who kept taking notes in the cabin, wrote
that he was listening to Jefferson Starship when the captain
came on to tell them the plane had been hijacked, and that they
must do exactly what was asked. The captain told them to stay
calm, the hijackers were fully armed, had a bomb on board, and
threatened to blow up the plane if they did not obey them.

While Flight 355 traveled over Canada, TWA officials in
Montreal radioed New York that a bomb and a message could
be found inside locker 5713 under Grand Central Station at
Lexington Avenue and 42nd Street.

At 9:01 p.m., Hank Dworkin picked up the phone in the
arson-explosion squad room and wrote down the details as they
were relayed to him. *Suspicious device at Grand Central.* The
seventeen men assigned to the bomb squad rotated partners, and
he was up, along with Brian Murray. Emergency Service was
dispatched, the area was cordoned off, and subway traffic halted
as police ripped the door of the locker from the hinges with a
claw tool.

Inside locker 5713 they found a Macy's shopping bag with
a pressure cooker inside. Its handle had been removed. After
attempting to fluoroscope the device, they found the metal

pot was impenetrable. Along with the shopping bag was an eight-page manifesto from Fighters for Free Croatia. "There is another bomb somewhere in New York City," the letter read. Print this manifesto in the *New York Times*, *The Chicago Tribune*, and *The Los Angeles Times*, and we will tell you where to find the second device. We want the world to help put a stop to the subjugation of the Croatian people, and we are willing to blow up an aircraft filled with innocent people to be heard."

Authorities diverted air traffic from New York City, halted all public transportation, put emergency tankers on hold at all local airports, and every precinct in the New York City Police Department had officers looking for suspicious packages.

Amid the crowd of police vehicles with flashing lights, Brian pulled up with Bertha, the bomb squad truck fitted with a basket that could take the impact of high explosives. It was the scene I had witnessed on television, the marquee of the Commodore Hotel seen just above the truck, Brian on one end of the pole, Hank on the other, the bomb balanced in the middle.

On the hijacked plane, passengers were strapped in their seats without recourse against the bombs Captain Carey told them were on board.

Zvonko and Julie Busic were composed as they sat in the seat facing the pilot. "We have a declaration we want printed in newspapers across the nation." He spoke in broken English, Julie adding a few words to make their demands clear.

"We also have leaflets in our luggage that we want dropped over key cities in America and Europe. We want the world to know about the atrocities being carried out by the Yugoslav government, the pillage and rape, entire villages leveled. We have pleaded for your government to become involved and no one has helped. There is nothing more we can do but try to convince the American people to come to our aid. This bomb, he pointed to the cylinders duct taped to his chest, has a timing device that will be activated if you do not do what we tell you. We want you to fly this aircraft over London and Paris and then to Croatia to drop the leaflets, and we want another plane to drop more leaflets over New York City and Los Angeles."

Captain Carey told the terrorists he would cooperate, but the aircraft didn't have enough fuel to fly across the Atlantic. It was intended for domestic use and had only enough fuel to fly to Chicago, where he would have refueled for the next leg of his flight.

If you try to drop papers from this aircraft they would get sucked into the engines, he told Busic. It cannot be done. He then promised he would notify the FAA to request a refueling stop and a second aircraft that could accomplish the task.

Dr. Brockman, the note-taker, wondered if they were French separatists. "The oily-skinned one walks the aisle, sticks of dynamite taped to his chest, detonator in his hand. 'Thirsty?' Julie Busic asked, approaching Dr. Brockman. 'Can I get you something?' Blue eyes shining, blonde hair turned up at the end, as if she hijacked the plane so she could play hostess."

They stopped in Newfoundland where the documents stashed in their suitcases were transferred to a 707 escort plane. They then flew to Montreal to refuel. There, Busic let out thirty-five passengers who feigned illness or had time constraints, "just to show some good will," he'd said. Julie stood by, watching each person file off. She whispered to one of the disembarking women, "I wish I were going with you."

Dr. Richard Brockman wrote: "They are taking me. I must write it all down. The thought of no more paper is as terrifying as the thought of no more time."

He then recorded the captain's words: "The hijackers have informed me that we are going to fly to London, Paris, and Croatia. They have not told me any further plans. The plane has been refueled . . . please extinguish all smoking material."

The Busics passed out leaflets for the passengers to read. "We have no intention of killing anybody. All we want is for our declaration to be published in American newspapers. We are not asking for difficult things. We want the world to recognize the injustices against our people—the people of Croatia."

Looking out the window, Dr. Brockman saw a mirage. " . . . an incredible sight. I want to be the pilot of that plane. She is just across from me, fifty yards, wing tip to wing tip. The pilot holds her back so she stays with us. My eyes run down her straight lines. I am falling in love with a plane. She tantalizes, teases, shows her belly and banks, climbs, falls, disappears, comes back. Wing tip to wing tip."

Once Busic noticed the French escort plane, he ran up and down the aisle yelling, "Pull the shade. Pull the shade." The craft and the passengers were now in the dark. They no longer knew whether it was day or night or where they were. A Catholic bishop on board took the microphone and led them in prayer.

In London, the plane circled in a holding pattern until the propaganda leaflets were dropped, then flew on to Paris. The Freedom Fighters were expecting the same course of action in France, but as the craft touched down at Charles de Gaulle Airport, French sharpshooters shot out the tires. They didn't want a plane that might explode to fly over their county. "It was a pretty rough landing," one of the passengers reported. "We were scared to death."

FLOODLIGHTS AT THE DEMOLITION SITE lit up the eastern part of the Bronx like Yankee Stadium. As Brian and Hank balanced the black kettle, Brian turned to his sergeant, Terry McTigue, and said, "I can smell the nitroglycerin." This was Terry's case, and he called the shots. In the best case scenario, the sergeant would contain the explosion and then examine the workings, but there wasn't time. There was a plane filled with Americans whose hijacker threatened to blow them up with a matching device, and they had to know the intricate details of the bomb in New York in order for the French bomb squad to safely take apart the duplicate they were told was on the aircraft.

THE BUSICS WAITED FOR CONFIRMATION, by a pre-arranged code, that the newspapers had printed their declaration. Authorities towed the plane to an airfield away from Charles De Gaulle Airport, flat tires bumping along the tarmac. There French police in bomb trucks with water cannons and hundreds of sharpshooters surrounded the aircraft. Inside the darkened plane they waited and waited, but in a breakdown of communication, there was no news that their demands had been met. The passengers were kept locked inside, authorities refusing to bring them food or drink or empty the toilets, which had begun to overflow.

"I am in my seat," Brockman wrote. "I am not sure how much time has gone by, whether it is dark out or light. I am not hungry, not thirsty, not tired, not hopeful, not fearful, not seeing, not hearing, not sensing."

At the disposal range at Rodman's Neck in the Bronx, Hank and Brian placed the device in a twenty-five foot crater, and Terry McTigue, former major in the U.S. Army Ordnance Corps, directed the two men to attach an activator to the wires on the pressure cooker and cover it with an explosion suppression blanket. When the wires were severed, the bomb would either explode, the pieces contained inside the bomb blanket, or be neutralized.

The plane sat on the runway for more than twelve hours. Passengers cried and pleaded for the hijackers to surrender, pleaded with the captain to force the newspapers to print the propaganda. They needed food and clean sanitary conditions. The smell of the overflowing restrooms was beginning to make them sick.

Desperate, Busic herded together the passengers and threatened to kill them. "We will blow up the plane unless authorities confirm the declaration has been printed."

Busic had not counted on the French refusing to cooperate.

He had not counted on hours and hours of stalled negotiations, and he made a final request: allow his wife to leave the plane with the co-pilot to confirm that the papers had printed the proclamation.

AT THE PIT, BRIAN SPOKE his last words to Inspector Behr: "We use a new cutter each time. They cost twelve bucks."

The team waited the requisite time, but the bomb did not detonate. As was their procedure, Brian Murray, Hank Dworkin, and Terry McTigue climbed back into the crater. That was when the bomb exploded, and when the confusion began. Why did the bomb suddenly explode? Had the wire cutter completely severed the wires? Had the severed wires somehow made contact? Was it sabotage? Human error?

When I begged Charlie to tell me how it happened, he said he didn't know. He said that it was all a matter of where the men were standing, that a dynamite blast is directional. Evidence showed that when the circuit completed and metal and sand shot out like a cannon, chewing up everything in its path, it was Brian, standing on the left, who took the full blow. Ragged chunks of the kettle ripped through him, severed his windpipe and tore holes in his body. McTigue, a few feet to the right, also took the force of the blast. Propelled into the air by the concussion, shards of debris whistled past and ripped off his fingers and pieces of his face. Hank, standing across from Brian, got the wind knocked out of him and he suffered cuts and bruises, temporary blindness and hearing loss, but remained intact.

I thought a hundred times about how it must have felt— the rumble and shock and deafening percussion as the ground rocked and the air transformed into a solid mass of black rain. Charlie had told me a dynamite blast is so violent you are knocked senseless, and when you wake up, if you wake up, you have no idea what happened. That means that Brian never knew what hit him, but I wondered if there was a moment when he did know, when he saw the flash and felt the panic. Did he think of me? His sons?

And what of McTigue, when he woke up to a ruined face and stumps for fingers, did he figure out what happened? As the highest-ranking expert in the New York City Police Bomb Squad, did he know what went wrong?

AT A TARMAC OUTSIDE OF Paris, Julie Busic and the co-pilot were allowed to get off the plane. When they were picked up in a van, the French police asked Julie how many terrorists were on the plane and were shocked when she said she was one of them. The police showed her proof that the declaration had been printed in the specified newspapers and she relayed to Captain Carey that their demands had been met.

Busic took the microphone: "You will be freed. You see, my friends, we have a cause, and we wanted the world to understand our cause, a cause of oppressed people. Now the world knows. I hope that you will support our aims. It is just; it is right. We will win, but it will be hard; a long, hard struggle is ahead for my people. I do not care what happens to me. They can kill me—cut me up into hundreds of little pieces, put me in jail for the rest of my life. They can do to me as they like, for the message is sent; I have done my work for my people. You are free to go now. There are no bombs, they are not real, just silly putty. We never intended to hurt you. And the pots, just clay, my friends. Just clay." And to the City of New York, Busic said, "there is no second device, only the one in locker 5713."

And so it was over for the hijacked passengers. Captain Carey took the microphone and asked for a round of applause for the Busics for their bravery and commitment. Somehow, during the course of the ordeal, the captain had been persuaded that the Freedom Fighters' cause was worthy of hijacking a plane.

At the time Captain Carey applauded the hijackers, he did not know that the bomb left in a New York City subway locker was filled not with silly putty, but real dynamite. He did not know that when the Busics placed that assembled device in the locker, they were sure it would not blow up and kill a cop who had recently celebrated his 27th birthday, blowing out candles with a wish that would never come true. The captain had yet to learn that the innocent-looking shopping bag made its trip to Grand Central Station on a warm afternoon where it sat unnoticed by hundreds of passersby until that young cop safely removed it and transported it to the sand pit in the Bronx. At the tmie he believed that while the Busics held captive his airplane filled with terrified passengers who were afraid those hours would be their last, that their actions were well-meaning, and that freedom for Croatian people was a justified reason for taking a plane hostage.

None of the hostages who applauded their hijackers knew that in a few months the sympathetic couple who held them hostage would be sentenced to life in prison for taking the life of a police officer, father of two little boys who dreamed of a picnic with their Daddy. The picnic his wife had already prepared. The one they would never share.

Captain Carey eventually learned the whole story of what happened in New York City while he placated the man and woman who held him captive on a French runway, but I never would. I continued to be plagued by the same questions. Why did a procedure the bomb squad had carried out hundreds of times unexpectedly fail? Why wouldn't McTigue talk to me? I wanted to know. But could I sue the NYPD as Charlie had suggested? I had grown up feeling invisible and had narrowly escaped a life of poverty and degradation. Who was I to sue the City of New York?

"COVER THESE NEWSPAPERS," MY MOTHER warned me when she moved her things into Brian's study the following weekend. "You don't want the boys seeing them."

I watched her looking askance at the notes I had taken

while she put away her teacup. As she unpacked a box of paper-backs that Timmy had helped move in, I realized that she had never outgrown turning her back on danger, pretending that perpetrators like her violent husband would disappear if she stopped looking at him. My mother didn't want to know how her son-in-law was killed. She wanted the whole thing to go away.

"Don't encourage her to read about those terrorists," I over-heard her say to Gracie one night. "Get her a good book."

It would be easier for me to just let go and make a new life for my sons and myself, but I knew that this was a legacy I could not bring into my life, this habit of hiding things, pushing them aside. Somewhere in the aftermath of the hijacking, it became clear to me that this kind of hiding was a seducer, something I needed to resist with everything in me. I could not dodge the truth of what the Busics had done or how that bomb exploded.

*The two most important days in your life are
the day you are born, and the day you find out why.*
— Mark Twain

Hiding

1954

I was seven when I first encountered my mother's propensity for hiding. Aunt Delia was coming to visit our Faile Street apartment. The yellowed organdy curtains that normally hung in the basement kitchen were getting a bath. The red refrigerator had been realigned, the kitchen chairs re-taped. Danny followed me as I swept the cellar floor. "Hold on to this cardboard," I instructed him. He squatted down so I could use it as a dustpan.

My mother put out a plate of donuts and her best teacups. Her lips were painted red and her apron was on its hook, her favorite blue dress in its place. "You play outside with your cousins," she told me. "I don't want them running around the cellar."

Our cousins, who lived in a house in Queens with a dock and a boat in their backyard, stood far enough away not to catch cooties. "My mother said not to touch anything," Frankie told us, and I thought about spitting on him when Johnny chimed in, "Let's play hide and seek."

In an effort to take them outside I said, "How about cracks in the sidewalk?" It was a game where you ran the length of the street without stepping on a crack, your body zigzagging like a crab.

Instead of listening to me, Frankie yelled, "You're it!" and was quick to take off for the back of the cellar.

"My mother said to stay outside," I yelled to him, but he kept going, so I ran outside and covered my eyes and counted as everyone but Danny scattered. He held onto my leg, sucked his thumb, and tried to see through his long blonde bangs.

"Eight, nine, ten," I called, ready to start my search, when Frankie ran from the cellar to the yard.

"There's a baby in there."

Johnny came from behind the stoop, Annie and Timmy from the next alleyway.

"Come see."

Frankie's face flushed as he hurried into the storage room. He had on the red high-top sneakers that were on the list of things I wanted but knew better than to ask for. We followed him. And there, among old brooms and buckets and stray pallets of wood, was our old baby carriage. When we poked our heads in we found a blue blanket. A tiny baby was wrapped inside.

"Who is this?" Frankie asked.

It probably belonged to one of the tenants, I thought, or maybe my mother was minding it for someone, but my face burned hot as though I were telling a lie.

"I don't know," I told him. The urge to pee made me squeeze my legs together.

Frankie ran into the kitchen and came back with Aunt Delia. "There's a real baby in the storage room." His voice was pitched high as a whistle. We all looked in at the baby, who kicked its feet and tried to focus its little blue eyes. Aunt Delia stared at the baby and then at me, like I had done something bad. She had the same face as my mother, the same blue eyes, but her hair was black. She smelled wonderful.

"Whose baby is this?" Delia asked. Her eyes were pinched together, making my stomach feel funny. And then she picked up the baby, apparently not concerned that it might throw up on her red dress. My mother stood at the door to the kitchen, her hands folded across her chest. "Who does this child belong to, Sarah?" Delia asked again.

My mother lifted her head, but I noticed the quiver in her chin. "His name is Patrick, and he's mine." She reached out and took the baby from her sister, burying her face in the blue blanket.

Aunt Delia cleared her throat. "I didn't know Tom still came around." She looked like she might cry too. "Sarah. Why didn't you tell me?" My mother shook her head, but she couldn't look at her sister who would not understand giving in to a husband who took her whether she protested or not.

"Can I hold him?" I reached out as Aunt Delia and my cousins gathered around, and my mother placed my newest brother in my arms.

"Hi Patrick." I touched his tiny nose. "You make eight."

MY MOTHER LEARNED TO HIDE what she loved early on. Back in their childhood in the '30s, it was Delia, older by two years, who had gotten pregnant first. When she and my mother were teens in a walk-up on West 80th Street that reeked of boiled cabbage, my mother had to pretend she was the good sister, wiping off the lipstick she put on after school, shivering at the thought of Papa finding out about Bernie, the boy she wanted to marry as soon as she graduated high school.

And then one day she risked stopping at the Star movie theater where a sign called for a ticket taker at $2.50 a day. "I'm eighteen," she lied to the manager, hoping he didn't notice her Cardinal Spellman uniform under her coat. "I can work on Saturdays and Sunday after church," she told him, not sure at all if her father would let her.

"Come around on Saturday," the manager told her, "and we'll try you out."

She couldn't wait to tell Delia, stuck at home with a big belly that had taken her freedom and shut down the subject of dating for her three sisters, so that Sarah had to sneak around to see Bernie. She tucked the pack of Pall Malls into the plaid skirt she thought made her look like the nuns who taught her at Cardinal Spellman, and opened the door to find her mother at the stove, the usual white apron covering the front of her flowered dress that came to her ankles.

The way my mother told it, her papa had been sitting in the over-stuffed chair in the living room with *The Daily Mirror* and his cigar, a glass of Schlitz with a head of white foam on the table in front of him. Her papa wasn't tall, but the farming back in Ireland had made him big and strong. With his wavy brown hair and round blue eyes, she told me he was often called handsome.

But that day she walked into the living room and told him, "I got a job, Papa." Her heart kicked in her chest. "It pays two dollars a day," she lied, "and all I have to do is take tickets at the movie theater on Saturday and Sundays." She thought the two dollars would persuade him, it was the depression after all, and she could put the other fifty-cents in her pocket. She didn't tell him that the most exciting part of the job was that during breaks she could see Bernie. After work he could sneak in the side door and save the price of the fifteen-cent ticket, and together they could watch Clark Gabel stride across the screen.

"I'll think about it," he said, and went back to his newspapers.

"He won't let you work at the movies," Delia told her later. "He's afraid you'll end up like me, pregnant and unmarried." When my mother told me this story, I pictured Delia giving her a little smirk, pushing her glossy black curls out of her eyes, and my mother's smugness, thinking she would never let herself get in Delia's situation, never let Bernie go all the way until they were married.

That Friday afternoon she had come straight home from school, dropped her books on the kitchen table, and braced for Papa's answer. He had stalled three days, and if he didn't say yes by tonight, the job would be lost. She stopped short when she saw a man standing in the living room with big ears and a cigarette burning low between his fingers. He was probably a friend from Papa's job as a house painter. But her father introduced her.

"This is Tom Martin," he said. "He would like to marry you."

My mother had looked more closely at the man, at his shiny suit hanging on his skinny frame. "This is surely the best thing," her father told her. "Tom will provide for you." She then turned toward the kitchen. "Mama?" But her Mama was suddenly very busy with the dishes.

Delia got pregnant, but it was Sarah who was forced to marry, doomed to a life with a stranger whose only redeeming trait was that he was Irish. Her parents didn't have to worry about Catherine, the oldest, who promised she was going to become a nun as soon as she was over the Tuberculosis that had plagued her since she was a child, or Maggie, who had joined the Navy to get out of the house.

"If you would rather the convent, Sarah, we can arrange that," her father had said later when they sat down for dinner. Papa and Tom painted houses together and sometimes stopped for a beer after work. Tom was 28 years old, had a job, an apartment in the Bronx, and would keep her from carrying on with that boy who her father knew walked her home from school.

A month later, Sarah wore a navy polka-dot dress and matching hat she borrowed from Delia and stood next to Tom Martin in front of a clerk at City Hall. Had she been more discreet with Bernie, my mother sometimes told me, everything would have turned out differently.

"But it's best not to think about the past," she told me again and again. "The past will break your heart faster than anything." She told me versions of this story many times in my childhood, sitting at the kitchen table, smoking cigarettes, her feet up after a long day at the automat. It seemed to act as some kind of apology or excuse for all the attention she never paid us. And I did feel sorry for my mother because I couldn't imagine what it must have been like to be married to Tom Martin—a man I hated before I was old enough to understand the contempt he felt for his wife and children.

To my father, we were five dollars a kid. On Wednesdays after school, Annie and I would pick up the child-support money. On our way through Grand Central, passersby did a double-take at two girls heading through the terminal, too young to walk around the city alone. But I was used to traveling by myself and had been riding the subways since I was old enough to read the station names.

42nd Street bustled with guests coming and going from the Commodore Hotel and commuters swarming down the stairs to the subway trains. We stood beneath the big Tiffany clock and waited for my father to come out of the Horn & Hardart automat on his cigarette break. The 42nd Street store was one of the first automats, opened in 1902, and one of my father's jobs, since he had quit house painting, was to stand behind a glass booth and hand out nickels for the slots that dispensed sandwiches and coffee that flowed from a brass lion's mouth. "Nickel thrower," my mother called him, "that's all he's good for."

Wind whipped at my skirt and I thought about the warm restaurant and the pie that came around on a carousel. But when my father crossed the street, he didn't bring us pie. He didn't even say hello. He lit up a Camel with yellow fingers and smoked as if we weren't there. Finally, he glanced at me, spit a fleck of tobacco from his tongue, and handed me four tens.

"I need carfare, too," I said, abandoning the idea of asking for pie. His mouth twisted into a grimace as he reached into his pocket, and he shoved two dimes at me. Then he jaywalked across 42nd Street and disappeared inside the revolving doors.

THERE WERE TIMES THAT THE cloak of invisibility served me well. So many times, I had watched my father's hands grab hold of my mother and squeeze until she was down on her knees, had listened as his smoke-ruined voice called her "slut," "whore," "bitch." But no matter how much Fleischmann's whiskey he drank or how many times he whipped off his belt, my father never touched me. For a long time, I wondered when my time would be up, until I realized he didn't see me. I was five dollars.

MY MOTHER'S PAPA, OLD AND bald by the time I met him, had also affirmed this idea that I was invisible. I remember going to his house in Queens for his birthday. He stood at the door and watched his daughter's eight children walk up the narrow walkway. He let my mother and Rose and Gracie in the door and then stopped in front of the rest of us, backing up the line.

"You sit on the top step," he told Corky, pointing to the flight of stairs leading to the bedrooms, "and you," he pointed to me, "sit two steps down, and the rest of you, whatever your names are, skip a step and sit down."

We each took our step—Corky, me, Annie, Timmy, Danny, and Patrick—and didn't move until he came back with a tray of six plates of birthday cake. He handed Corky a plate and doled out the cake to the rest of us on his way down.

"Don't spill anything," he said as he walked away.

We could hear our aunts chatting, cousins running around the house, but never close enough to see. Finally, I took a bobby pin from my hair and scratched the flowers off the wallpaper so they would know I was there.

Nothing should be out of the reach of hope.
—Oscar Wilde

Juxtaposition

My mother would have liked me to move on with my life, but I couldn't do that until I had answers. The trial date for the Busics hovered like an impending storm, but when the district attorney asked me to meet in his office, I thought I would find resolution to the questions that left me troubled.

It was a few weeks before Christmas when I sat in David Trager's office. I could almost feel the Busics across the way in federal lockup, a block from Foley Square. While I waited for him to make himself comfortable behind his desk, I tried to steady my heartbeat. The room seemed smaller than I expected, overheated, crowded with papers, books, and files piled everywhere.

"Your presence at the trial is important," the district attorney told me. His salt-and-pepper hair and wire-rimmed glasses gave him a formidable look, and I was glad I wouldn't have to answer his questions on the witness stand. "You should be in the courtroom as a show of support for your husband and for the NYPD."

He told me the Busics had support from the Croatian community, groups who raised money for their defense. "They've been deluged with mail and gifts from sympathizers who congratulate them for their bravery and sacrifice."

It galled me that there were people who sanctioned blowing up a cop, who thought of the bombing as an accident, a small sacrifice to pay for their cause. *It wasn't the fault of the Croatian Freedom Fighters that the bomb went off,* they reasoned, *the bomb on the plane was fake, so the judge would be lenient. There were so many worse criminals in the city, the PLO, the FALN.*

"Will they get out on bail?" The thought paralyzed me.

"No. They're being charged with hijacking which resulted in the death of a police officer." I squeezed my hand to control the shaking, and the sharp edge of the engagement ring I refused to take off dug into my skin. "That will keep them in prison for many years. Now," Trager took out a legal pad, "tell me about your husband."

I wanted to tell him about Brian's eyes—magnetic blue ringed with dark lashes—about the kindness he showed people I crossed the street to avoid, that he hated beans, and thought tardiness a lack of respect. I wanted to tell him what a great father he was. How he fixed the boys' breakfast and lunch while I commuted to Manhattan, and pushed metal trucks over the floor and made up endless stories to hear them laugh. I had stored up perfect memories, one after another, which was how I imagined loved ones remembered the dead, sharp edges smoothed, complexities ironed out.

But the DA couldn't talk about perfect memories in a court-room, so instead I told him about Brian Murray who served in Vietnam, the bomb expert, trained to dismantle explosives by the United States Air Force, the FBI, and the New York City Police Department, a man who could detangle a potentially fatal scrabble of wires without breaking a sweat. A man with steady hands and faith in God, who had simply followed orders when he stepped into the pit at Rodman's Neck.

Trager wrote on his pad without looking up, my words just information he would add to his trial notes. Then he put down his pen and looked at me.

"I know this is difficult for you, Mrs. Murray, but I want you to know that I'll do everything in my power to bring the people responsible for your husband's death to justice."

"Will they get the death penalty?" I asked.

Trager told me the death penalty wasn't mandatory in all hijacking cases. After carefully considering the law that mandated the death penalty, he did not believe this case would apply, as the evidence could not establish depraved indifference, the intent to kill.

"The maximum sentence is twenty-five to life." And that meant that Busic would be eligible for parole in ten years, and Julie in eight. "It will be up to the judge's discretion." Then he stood, signaling the end of our meeting.

THE CITY WAS DRESSED FOR Christmas, with fake-bearded Santas ringing Salvation Army bells, wreaths strung up on lampposts, dazzling store windows, and even the air felt like Christmas. I took the subway to midtown, stepped into FAO Schwarz on a whim, and bought the Christmas display with a cowboy and Native American village. The price tag was more than I had ever spent on the boys for anything, but I wanted it for them, for me.

I remembered Brian telling me how, when he was a little boy, his living room would be filled with gifts for the five kids: bicycles, dolls, rocking horses, games, clothing, anything a child could wish for. His face had been a mixture of emotions when he told me how they would rip into the endless piles of presents.

"But it was only temporary. As soon as my father left for work the next day, the room would be cleared out, the bicycles gone, the dolls and toys vanished. 'Christmas is over,' my mother would tell us."

As a boy, he dreamed about the presents that disappeared in the same way our sons now dreamed about their father, only to wake up to our new normal, a life without Daddy.

When I got home that night, the house smelled of the wood-burning fireplace, and my mother was settled on the couch with a cup of tea and a romance novel. The lights on the

Christmas tree gave a festive air to the house, but all I could think about was Christmas without Brian by my side to watch the surprise on Keith's face when he saw the fire engine he asked Santa for. My head pulsed with pain as I remembered the DA's words. Ten years. I couldn't picture my life in ten years. I couldn't even picture it in one.

My mother had called Timmy to put up the tree. When we were little, Timmy and I dragged a tree from Southern Boulevard to Faile Street every Christmas. The old guy we called Pumpkin Head finally gave us one nobody would pay for. No teeth and a caved-in face with a cigarette stuck in his mouth, Pumpkin Head would tell us again and again to come back later, but we stood around until he got tired of telling us to get lost. "Here ya go," he would snarl through cigarette smoke, and shove the skinny tree at us. "Don't come back next year."

This year, with his new wife Jean, Timmy had come all the way from the Bronx with the tree tied to the roof of his Chevy Nova, and I felt grateful to him for making the house look alive.

In the kitchen, the yapping of our new puppy, Morty, increased the pain in my head. "Pipe down," I pleaded with the cocker spaniel. Morty Moot Mope, after the rhyming puppet from Sesame Street, had been a concession on my part, and since we brought him home there had not been a peaceful moment. The grief books told me not to do anything drastic in the months just after a death, but I stopped working, bought a puppy, invited my mother to move in with us, sold the house in Rockville Centre, and moved to Northport in the span of a few months.

When I thought back to the day we moved to Northport, my loss felt compounded. My mother and Gracie packed Brian's clothes. "Give them to someone who can use them," I told my mother, and looked away when Danny walked past with Brian's jackets and slacks still on hangers. Then I had taken a last look at the den where the couch we made love on was still outlined in dust. Timmy, Danny, and Patrick had already lifted furniture from the rooms that held the weight of our life together.

"Goodbye," I whispered as I closed the door behind me.

Our new Northport neighborhood smelled of hickory smoke and falling leaves, and the house seemed to be waiting for two little boys to bring laughter to its empty rooms. But Keith had sobbed.

"I can't find Daddy here." He ran to the window and watched my brothers pull away in the moving truck. "How will he find us?"

Now Keith and Chris were sitting at the kitchen table, leafing through a stack of comics Timmy brought with the tree, eating the SpaghettiOs my mother made for them.

"Hi Mom," Keith said. His face had lost that open, happy smile, and I thought again of the Busics in a holding cell, just a train ride away.

That night, Gracie melted wax for homemade candles as the boys sat mesmerized. I didn't have the heart to say what I thought, that the wax made a big mess, that the candles would burn down in minutes, that the kitchen smelled like burnt rope. Instead, I showed them the early Christmas present and the four of us got down on the living room rug and set up the village.

At bedtime, Keith snuggled under the comforter, a shock of red hair the only sign he was in the bed; Chris curled up in his footy pajamas in a big-boy bed to avoid any more stunts he devised trying to climb out of his crib. I kissed them both, my lips lingering on their soft skin. I stood at their window for a few moments, listening to their little boy sounds and thinking about the Christmas before when Brian had worked a four-to-twelve and I waited for him to share a glass of the eggnog I made for the family dinner the next day. It was two in the morning when we finally finished wrapping presents, and I watched as he folded the triangle of Santa paper just so, trying not to let his big bomb-squad thumbs get in the way. The stereo was playing Christmas carols on low, and we had fallen asleep, my head on his chest, all the Christmas presents around us, one of the cookies Chris left out for Santa still in Brian's hand.

Now, a wet snow fell and disappeared as soon as it hit the ground. Next door, a rectangle of light hit the stone walk. A minute later my neighbors appeared. The wife was carrying a red Christmas package and wearing a fur coat. I could hear laughter through the cold pane of glass, and then her husband picked her up and carried her down the path to their car, like a bride.

I thought about our visit to see Santa a few days before. When Santa asked what they would like, Keith asked for a fire truck. Chris said, "I want my Daddy back." Watching the slick snowfall and listening to my boys' breathing, a shiver ran through me. Soon I would be face-to-face with Zvonko Busic, the man who haunted my dreams, and Julie Busic, the mysterious woman who I thought about more than I would like to admit.

Over time, from library research and the files Charlie brought to me, I learned she had been born Julienne Schultz in the quaint little town of Gearhart, Oregon. Her father was a professor of classical Greek, her mother a librarian. She was the oldest of four, the only girl, most doted upon.

I not only envied Julie's childhood and the opportunities she had, I thirsted for them. I could almost taste her life, breathe the fresh Oregon air. As a girl, I would have gladly traded places with her, lived in the room I imagined she had all to herself— filled with books and school trivia—had parents who read my homework and prepared for my future.

How could anyone in her right mind decide that wasn't good enough? How could anyone throw it all away on a country that was so far away that most Americans couldn't even locate it on a map? I thought about what Gracie would have done with the life Julie had been given and was sure she would have followed her dream to become an airline hostess, and not become a junkie who would never rise above the memory of that first hit of nirvana. I was sure I would have made more of my own life too.

Something must have gone wrong in Julie's young life. Perhaps it was three brothers who usurped her position as an only child, but that didn't seem a clear reason for this upper-middle class American girl to disparage and disown her country. Perhaps she sought a more adventurous place than Gearhart, a more significant life in a foreign country. Still, that didn't explain her eerie trip down a terrorist's rabbit hole. The juxtaposition of what she had been brought up with and what she had done filled me with rage and envy.

DOWNSTAIRS, GRACIE'S LAUGHTER BROUGHT ME into the living room where she was cleaning up the cowboy village. A row of tampons in their plastic cases were lined up in front of a teepee.

"What the heck?" I looked to Gracie, who laughed again.

"Keith said they were cannons."

I laughed along with my sister, thinking my son very clever.

Out the back door, I watched my mother standing on the deck in her coat, a cigarette in her hand, her once-shiny red hair cropped short and combed with her fingers instead of a brush. She had given up her apartment in the Bronx to move to Northport. The country, she called it, where she couldn't call her friends to have a few beers after work and where she had to put on a coat to smoke a cigarette.

She came inside smelling of cigarettes and picked up a dish-towel to dry the dinner dishes. I tried to think of her as a young girl, kicking up her heels at the Irish step-dance lessons she told me she took with her sisters, but saw instead that vein running down her leg, like a twisted river that cuts a map.

"Leave the dishes, Mom. I'll do them."

She folded the dishtowel over the oven handle. She didn't want me to attend the trial, but asked Gracie to help her while I was gone. When she walked over to hug me, she whispered, "I love you, sweetheart."

I was twenty-eight years old and thought I had long ago given up the need to hear those words, but as soon as they were spoken I hugged her tight. "I love you too."

She stepped back and pushed her glasses up so she could see me better. *Sweetheart?* The word stayed in the room.

"Good night, Mom."

I gave her smooth cheek a kiss. She held on to the bannister as she walked up the stairs and looked back at me, the child who would now take care of her.

Gracie and I stayed up late into the night, a beer for her, a glass of chardonnay for me. "Trager said the trial could take weeks." I watched her take a sip of beer. "And I have to be there every day." I told her about the Busic supporters, the gifts, the idea that they were heroes to their countrymen.

She nodded when I told her about the likelihood that Julie would spend no more than eight years in prison. She grew pensive and stared at something I couldn't see. She had listened to the stories I read to her about Julie without saying much, and in some strange way, I thought she identified with Julie. Not the crime Julie committed, but the daring defiance of Julie's actions was something Gracie understood.

She put down her beer and looked at me with those pretty blue eyes. Finally, she nodded. "Well, promise me this, you'll do something nice for yourself when this trial is over." She said it with a ferocity I hardly recognized. "Go to college like you always wanted. Make a new life for you and the boys."

And just like when we were little girls, the world lit up with her words, her steady belief that little Kathy could be anything she chose.

"I'll study writing," I said with surety. With the addition of Social Security and my mother's help, I realized I might be able to make college work. It had always been a dream, and now I could take a few classes when the boys were in school. "I'll write a story about you," I told her, remembering the promise I made long ago.

Gracie laughed. "You'll have more than me to write about," she assured me.

After a while, we moved around the house and turned off the lights. But we left the Christmas tree glittering in the night.

*The price of anything is the amount
of life you exchange for it.*
— William Faulkner

The Trial

Brian had been gone five months when DA Trager called and told me the trial would begin. I sat in the back of the courtroom, the only one to support Brian. Gracie had taken some vacation time to spend with her newest boyfriend Billy, and my mother was with the boys. I had thought of calling Charlie to join me, but lately he avoided my calls. He didn't want to talk about the question I couldn't stop asking: with a bomb squad so qualified and experienced, why had the bomb exploded? I had to find out what happened, as not knowing felt like I was suffocating. Perhaps I would learn something from the trial.

From the back of the courtroom, I watched as dozens of Croatian supporters crowded the benches. They were there to support their champions, who had forfeited their freedom for the liberation of their country. Then I saw *them*, the Busics, sitting as close as lovebirds. Although I expected to see them, it hit me hard, and I felt a tremor inside that left me weak. Zvonko Busic, mangy and dressed in black, looked like what he looked like in all the pictures I had seen of him so far: a terrorist.

But Julie, his wife, had lace on the cuffs of her white blouse and a perfect mantle of blonde hair falling across the middle of her back. Just as I was studying her, she turned in her seat and looked back, her eyes finding mine. There was an imperceptible change in her face. Did she know me? I sat straighter on the hard bench, my bra strap digging into my shoulder, and I remembered Paul's words, *Unsuitable for viewing*. Suddenly I was glad the DA insisted I come. I wanted Julie to see me. I wanted to haunt her dreams, to plague her thoughts as the bomb tearing into Brian had mine.

I listened as the testimony droned on for hours. The FBI, the CIA, and the NYPD testified to the hijacking. The defense presented their case to the jury. I heard witness after witness praise the Busics' bravery, the sacrifice they made to call attention to the atrocities of a country that wasn't even Julie's.

I read that sympathizers called Julie a heroine, a saint, and a symbol, wrote poems in her honor and raised money for her defense. Things just went wrong, they said. It was unfortunate that the safe bomb wasn't safe after all. The officer's death was collateral damage.

Every afternoon the press filled the courthouse stairs, creating a gauntlet as I tried to make my way to my car.

"Do you plan to be in the courtroom when Busic is sentenced?" Chuck Scarborough, New York's most recognized anchor asked me.

"I'll be there when the judge takes away his freedom and will ask to be kept informed of his whereabouts," I said. "I want to know where he is for the rest of his miserable life."

"Busic claims it wasn't his fault the bomb exploded," another reporter asked. "Do you think he should be held accountable?"

"Busic made the bomb," I told him. "He packed eight sticks of dynamite into a pressure cooker and left it in a public area. You cannot design a bomb not to explode. By its very nature, dynamite is unstable, and there is always a chance of explosion with something so precarious." Flashbulbs went off everywhere. Two-dozen microphones were held in front of my face. "He is responsible. He should be made to pay for my husband's death with life in prison."

At night, after I put the boys to bed, I sat at the dining room table with our new puppy sleeping beside me and read the newspapers. Sources reported that Busic believed they would be tried in European courts, where the system was more lenient. He was surprised when they were extradited to New York where they would face harsher sentences, but the press was not at all sure harsher sentences were coming, given the overwhelming support they were enjoying.

THE DAY McTIGUE TESTIFIED ABOUT the explosion, his presence hung like a pall over the courtroom, his fragmented face a reflection of what Brian might have looked like, had he survived. On the witness stand he droned on in terms so technical, I could barely follow.

When it was Charlie's turn, he read the words from the official report. He looked tired, his mustache a bit too thick, his wide collar shirt and plaid jacket a bit out of trend. Without glancing my way, he told the courtroom that the device was designed to explode, regardless of a safety switch. All proper precautions were taken.

Finally, Julie was called to the stand. Her owl glasses distorted her pretty face. She kept her gaze fixed on the back of the room, and if she knew anyone in the audience, she didn't let on. Her parents? Brothers? The wife of the police officer she had been accused of killing? She was a statue. Impervious.

The defense lawyer made her seem like a reluctant participant who went along with the hijacking to support her husband, and for Croatia, a country she had come to love. I found myself sitting on the edge of my seat while she spoke. I wanted her to suffer, to hate her, but something about her intrigued me.

Why did she do it? What role did she play in planning the hijacking and building the bomb? Did she shop for the pressure cooker, and then sit by her husband's side while he assembled the dynamite? Did she type the letter of demands? Did she choose the locker to store the bomb, drop in the coins, and reassure herself that the eight sticks of dynamite were safe?

But she did not reveal any details, and said over and over that she was not a willing participant. "I never intended to be part of this hijacking," she testified. "I went along with my husband because I thought I was pregnant and feared he would be killed before I gave birth." Momentarily, watching her, I was shocked by this revelation, but as she stepped down from the stand, I understood it was a legal ploy.

In the end, the defense attorney claimed Busic hijacked the plane out of "psychological necessity, not free choice." His psychiatrist testified that Busic was in an abnormal state when he allegedly committed air piracy, homicide, and other criminal acts. "He was psychologically incapable of committing the offenses he was charged with, and this abnormal mental state was so exaggerated that it prevented him from exercising free will." These details did not shock me as did Julie's testimony. Instead, they sickened me. It's not my fault, Busic claimed, exploiting a childish exuse for an appaling crime.

On the day of the summation the courtroom was packed, this time with a bevy of NYPD there to hear a cop killer pronounced guilty. The DA spoke for hours, during which I think I fell asleep with my eyes open, so weary of the interruptions and objections.

Then, after five weeks and nearly fifty witnesses, the jury made their decision.

The Busics stood when the judge read the verdict: Guilty of aircraft piracy. Julie let out a whimper. Guilty of aircraft piracy resulting in the death of police officer Brian J. Murray.

"Yes," I cried out, but no one heard me, as the courtroom erupted with cries of disbelief. I wondered what these people thought, that they would get away with taking, or borrowing, as Busic put it, a plane, and making a bomb that could have killed so many more people?

Twenty-five to life. Julie bowed her head when the sentence was read. Trager had said that meant eight years. Only eight years in prison to think about the death of my husband.

ON THE train ride home I watched the city pass in a blur. It seemed like ages ago I had been in the DA's office, talking about the trial. I had felt a certain buoyancy then. Even if I had to sit through their trial, I would finally know the truth of what happened, I would finally understand why that bomb had exploded.

But for five weeks I sat in a cold courtroom listening to the hijackers tell their story, and I still didn't know why the bomb exploded. They insisted it was built not to explode. Charlie, the only one on the bomb squad who had ever talked to me, had been avoiding my calls since I phoned to tell him I moved to Northport. "Yeah. Good," he told me. "Get away from the memories." I could hear it in his voice: *not her again.*

Maybe, I thought, as the train passed the 59th Street Bridge, he and the bomb squad had not talked to me because they wanted the Busics to receive the full brunt of the blame. But now that they were sentenced, I wondered if he would finally reveal what he knew.

WHEN I GOT HOME, THE house was empty. My mother had taken the boys to the science museum, and without even thinking about it, I picked up the phone and dialed the bomb squad. "A friend," I told a voice I didn't recognize after I asked for Charlie and realized they had replaced Brian.

Charlie sounded distant, wary, so I skipped the pleasantries. "I read a report in the paper that the wire-cutter activated the bomb just as the men were approaching." I came across an article at the library by chance; I sometimes spent whole afternoons there when the boys were in pre-school, the quiet room comforting. The words Bomb Squad had stared out from the screen at me. "Is that what happened, Charlie?"

I could hear him breathing, someone talking in the background. I pictured the cluttered office with photographs on the wall of the two bomb squad detectives killed at the '39 World's

Fair, and pictured a new one of Brian, unveiled in a ceremony I wasn't invited to. "Are you there?"

Finally, he said, "I don't know, Kathy. I told you the investigation was inconclusive."

I thought the investigation told them everything they needed to know about that wire-cutter. But now, with the trial over, I understood he wasn't ever going to tell me. "I don't want to file a lawsuit, Charlie, but I have to know why that bomb exploded. I spent weeks at that trial, and I still don't know. Please give me something."

"Again, Kathy, we don't know."

He couldn't see the tears, but he could hear the desperation in my voice as I stood up and steadied myself against the kitchen counter. "Why didn't you insist on bomb suits?" I asked. "I read those suits have saved lives." It wasn't a new discussion, but I needed something to grasp on to, a reason to open the dialogue.

"I told you already, the suits aren't required equipment." I knew there was a budget freeze and setbacks from the Knapp Commission, which gave the NYPD a black eye, but that didn't mean the men who put their lives on the line weren't entitled to protection. "They're still in the development stage. We're looking into them."

A swell of frustration brought fresh tears. It had been months of these phone calls, me desperate for answers, Charlie dodging them.

"Well, that settles it," I told him. "As you suggested, I'm going to sue the city to find out why the bomb went off and why the department didn't provide safety equipment." The words made me feel strong.

"You do what you have to," Charlie told me. "I'm sorry."

I felt the thin thread that held our friendship together snap. I put down the receiver without saying goodbye.

That night, I thought about all the repercussions that would come from suing the city. All the trouble a lawsuit would cause. It would end any chance of hearing from the bomb squad again, and a history Brian and I shared together would be lost. Ironically, if I filed a lawsuit, I would be saying the NYPD, not the hijackers, held the blame for Brian's death. Which wasn't quite true. I believed they were both responsible. But in the justice system, unlike life, there could be only one villain.

SHORTLY AFTER THAT PHONE CALL I went to see my attorney. Phil DeCicco was an old friend, and while I knew we could sit in his office for hours and talk about the times we got together to drink margaritas, those days were over. I was here on official business. Phil would represent me in a multi-million dollar suit against the City of New York. The lawsuit wasn't about money, it never even occurred to me to sue for money, but Phil informed me when I said I didn't want the money that, "Ultimately, everything is about money."

His office was high above 42nd Street. The city was quiet at that height, gleaming and invincible, straining toward the sky. Below was the Horn & Hardart where my father stood behind a row of carousels, shoving wrapped sandwiches into vacant slots. I could see Grand Central, where Brian spent his last hours. I turned my back on a view Phil paid a fortune to look at; I did not want to look at the sorrow that street held.

When I asked him if I was doing the right thing, he nodded, gravely. "You are entitled to know what happened, and this is the only way to do it. The Department has tied your hands by keeping the truth from you. The finest bomb squad in the world had no safety equipment, and you can change that by exposing them in a court of law. You are absolutely doing the right thing." He leaned back in his soft leather chair.

"When you called I started thinking about that party last summer when Brian told us a story about the FBI agent who lost his pants." Phil's aviator glasses and big mustache made him look more like a motorcycle cop than an attorney. He laughed softly. "He had everyone in hysterics."

I nodded. "He had a hundred stories," I said. "Keith

keeps asking me to tell him some, but I don't remember them anymore. Not one."

After I left his office, I crossed Fifth Avenue to the steps of the library where I used to watch Brian direct traffic when he first went on the job. I could still see him with a whistle in his mouth, his hands signaling cars to clear the busy intersection. The cold air tasted different, the afternoon sun too bright, and the memory faded, the wind reminding me I was staring at an empty space.

*The beautiful thing about learning is that
no one can take it away from you.*
— B. B. King

The City that Raised Me

Suing the City felt akin to suing my mother. The city had raised me. New York City was *The Daily News, The Post,* and police sirens. It was kids playing potsy and slug, public transportation—a pop down subway stairs and ten cents and twenty minutes later—a pop up on Canal for dumplings, or Bleecker for a used copy of *Gone With the Wind.* There wasn't a lot of room to plant a garden, and a swim in the East River was taking your life in your hands, but it was a good place to get your street smarts. I knew which gangs to cozy up to and which to avoid, just how much pot to smoke to look cool but not get too stoned, and which boys were only looking for one thing. New York taught me you could be a star. West 42nd Street was known for burlesque shows and hookers of every shape and size, catcalling from the sidewalk.

New York! Where you could take acting lessons from Telly Savalas. Telly had yet to hit his stride, but he was famous enough to draw a bunch of teenage girls who thought they could act. On Saturdays, we ducked around prostitutes in glo-orange leotards and leopard jackets and walked up the rickety steps to Telly's Tenth Avenue studio. A permanent cigarette hung from his lips, and he squinted through the smoke as he gave commands to clumsy wannabes. He told us he knew

Buddy Holly, who had been killed in a plane crash. He sang a few bars of "Peggy Sue," and we swooned over the dark-haired hunk we believed would land us in Hollywood.

New York brought me Mary Lin too, and through her, I would learn the power of the NYPD, which would later come back to haunt me when I decided to sue the city.

Every Sunday the streets of Chinatown teemed with Chinese and Jewish and Spanish and foreign-looking people who spoke languages I had never heard.

Mary's father Calvin told us he brought half his Chinese village to New York, and he seemed related to everyone, the store clerks where he bought congee and Lychee nuts, and the fishmonger who sold him stinky fish with eyes that stared out at me. Calvin's white shirt was starched and stiff around the collar, the sleeves rolled up to his elbows, his arms hairless and red from the hot iron he used in his Chinese laundry. He added Dragon's Beard candy to the mesh shopping bag, told us to save it for the ride home, and let us poke chopsticks into the dish of octopus swimming in fish sauce, lick them clean, and poke them into mu-shu pork, while waiters brought steaming platters of dumplings and chicken in velvety sauces.

"Last one back to Boomie's candy store is a rotten egg," Mary would yell. It was the middle of the night. Every store on our street was closed except for Calvin's Chinese Hand Laundry, where the lights stayed on well past midnight, when Calvin did the ironing. I didn't wonder if he slept, I was only happy Mary and I were awake when everyone else was asleep.

"Let's race," she yelled, and we headed for the corner, the wheels of our roller skates sparking on the black concrete at 2:00 a.m. It was still warm, and we wore shorts and midi-blouses tied in a knot so our bellies showed.

We shot past her father's store where he sprayed each shirt with starch and ran an iron that weighed more than me over the coarse material, steam floating up, giving the store a clean smell. He folded and put a paper tag with a sticky edge around each pile, then ripped a sheet of brown paper from a giant roll and wrapped it around the shirts, crimping the edges and tying the package together like a present, breaking the string with his thick red fingers. We took a break from roller-skating to help him stack the shirts on the shelves in number order.

"Race you to Boomie's," Mary yelled a second time, and we took off again. Our skates scraped along the empty side-walk, until I hit a bump and fell down on my hands and knees, blood beading up on the scrapes. Through the open door of the laundry, Calvin took one look and made a face.

"Sit down, Caddy. I fix." I loved how he said my name and watched as he ran a soft cloth soaked in warm water over the scrapes, put on a Band-Aid, and made me as good as new. I looked out the storefront window and ate the piece of red lico-rice he had handed to me, surprised when a black sedan with a running board pulled up to the curb and two men got out. It was there in the warm streets of late night New York that I learned justice could have a strange and sometimes violent face.

"This is a raid," the policemen called out as they walked into the store. Detectives, I thought, dressed in suits. "Sit over there," they told Mary and me, and we quickly obeyed. One had on a green bow tie, his face long and thin. The other one was heavier with a barbershop mustache and a meaty face. They pulled Calvin's carefully packaged brown paper-wrapped bundles from the shelves.

"What do you want?" Calvin placed his hands flat on the ironing surface like he needed support, his face bright red.

"We know you take numbers, so give us the name of your bookie and we won't destroy your store." The mustached cop looked down at Mary and me like we might know who the customers were that gambled with Calvin. My licorice hung limp in my hand.

"I don't have books." Calvin's heavy hands knotted into fists. "Get out of my store."

After swiping everything from the shelves, the beefy detective dumped over the coffee cans with the brown slips of paper containing the names he was looking for. He looked at the Chinese characters before tossing them to the side. "We're watching you," he told Calvin and stepped on a shirt, leaving his dirty footprint behind. Mary's red hair bow had come untied, her face pale, and I watched her reach out to pick up the dirty shirt.

For some reason, it was this scene that came back to me after I filed the lawsuit. My attorney said he would put us on the calendar, but it would be a while before the actual trial took place, and so it hung over me as I started my first year of college classes. My mother had assimilated into our lives, turning a blind eye to my court case and giving me the opportunity to attend classes. The boys went to school, fatherless. Late into the night I wrote papers for my creative writing class and wondered who I thought I was, going up against the authority of one of the most powerful cities in the world.

New York was where I found my first job as a secretary at the Warner Brothers offices in the Pan Am Building in midtown. There, I watched movie trailers with sound tracks that didn't match moving parts and took dictation as part of a pool of stenographers. I saw Paul Newman in the hallway and he said hello to me, and Faye Dunaway in the ladies room, who didn't. It was day after day of dictation and typing and I itched to write a script and hand it to my boss, but when I asked if he would be interested, he said they had professionals who wrote their scripts.

I said yes when Roger from the video department asked me to a holiday party. There I met Fiona Ryan, boy crazy, bouncy, bubbly, and fun. "I work for an Irish import company on Fortieth off Fifth," she told me. I liked her right away. "It's not as glamorous as Warner Brothers, but the pay is good, and the people are nice."

She put in a good word with the president, Harry Banks, and I scored an interview for an administrative position that paid double what I made at Warner Brothers. Harry looked like a pitbull, shorter than me by two inches. "Take this down," he said in a British accent, nodding to the pad he pushed across his desk. He sized me up, now a tall redhead.

He talked, and I took down his words in shorthand. When I looked up he was staring at the pad.

"How fast can you take dictation?"

I had no idea, really, but said the first thing that came to my mind, "How fast can you talk?" I thought it was a mistake, but his laughter was a surprise, hearty, from the gut.

"When can you start?" I was startled, had to restrain myself from doing a little dance. He said, "I'm happy to have someone who's not afraid to speak up."

Would I have become that way, someone willing to speak up, I often wondered, if I hadn't defied my mother by staying in school and carving out a career different than another number at Horn & Hardart? Fiona and the friends I made through work didn't see through me as my mother always had, so that when I met Brian, I recognized in him that same quality. Like them, he knew how to not just see me, but hold me and love me, until I believed that I really was the treasure he believed me to be. But even though I made my way from the Bronx to Manhattan and had gained a certain confidence, I wondered who I thought I was, going up against the authority of one of the most powerful cities in the world.

So we beat on, boats against the current,
borne back ceaselessly into the past.
— F. Scott Fitzgerald, *The Great Gatsby*

Fading Memories

It was an unseasonably warm day in June and I had just gone to lunch with Harry Banks, who ordered rich cream linen wallpaper from Belgium after I mentioned I was thinking of linen for the living room walls. It felt as though gifts like these were sliding unassumingly and easily into my hands lately, as though the universe suddenly felt shameful about all that it had taken away and wanted to begin to bring some of it back. My acceptance of these gifts was tentative, almost cloistered. I wanted to believe again, but my trust was still shy. At home, I opened the sliding glass doors and settled on the sofa to work on an essay about the role of witchcraft in women's literature.

I can't remember now what made me glance up at the leather-bound photo albums on the shelves across from me. But because I had ordered the room perfectly, I saw almost immediately they were out of order. 1974 was after 1976. I put my essay on the floor and pulled out 1976. The pages smelled like hot dusty floorboards, and I flipped through photos of Keith, blowing out four candles on his birthday cake, a snap of Chris in his PJs attempting to escape out the back door, and me, pregnant with Keith, a belly so big it looked like I was having twins.

But when I got to the page where Brian should have been posing outside the camper on that day, dressed in cut-offs and plaid shirt, smiling at the camera like it wasn't the last photo he would ever pose for, the photograph was missing. All that was left was a blank space. And when I flipped the page, the next picture slots were empty, too. I kept flipping through the pages for the one of Brian's twenty-seventh birthday in a family hug, or the one on the Fourth of July with the four of us in front of Op-Sail and the parade of ships on the Hudson, Brian in a suit and tie, after he had worked the night with Charlie sweeping the site for bombs. I turned the pages back as though by magic, the photos would reappear. And when they did not, I felt sick, almost faint. I kept the photo album in front of me, the silent blank pages like a stretching emptiness that haunted that afternoon.

"Did you take pictures of Brian out of the albums?" I asked when my mother came home that night. The boys were in bed, teeth brushed, stories read. I was standing at the sink, doing the last of the dinner dishes.

"Yes, I did." She walked out the sliding door, and I heard her light a cigarette. Drying my hands quickly on the dishtowel, I followed her out.

"Why?" Her hand shook when she raised the Pall Mall to her mouth. "Mom?" She turned to face me, and I saw the tears in her eyes.

"Because I thought they made you too sad." She had styled and sprayed her hair and was wearing a low-cut black dress and the matching three-inch heels she favored because they showed off her long legs. It reminded me again of those days when she was getting ready to go to work, me sitting on the bathtub, wishing for a little piece of her.

"I watched you go through those pictures time and again, Kathy." She inhaled smoke from her cigarette. I looked down at the album I had carried outside with me. "And knew how much it hurt you to see Brian." Her face, pale and lovely in the moonlight, was starting to look older, worn. "So I got rid of them."

The hurt was so strong that I had trouble saying the words. "Those photos didn't make me sad, Mom, they made me happy to remember the wonderful times we shared."

I saw her swallow, but she didn't say anything else. She just looked out at the trees, smoking, as though I wasn't even there.

WHEN I OPENED MY EYES the next morning the thought of those lost photos came to me immediately, as though they had been waiting for me while I slept. The hollowness they left behind felt almost physical. I closed my eyes and thought of my mother, two years before, sitting on the chair beside my bed. Even in the midst of my terrible grief, I had some shining splinter of hope that this was a new mother who would be there for me, able to single me out when I needed her, to tell me that she loved me.

It occurred to me in a flash how strangely lucky I was. Somehow I knew to be hungry for her love, somewhere in me I knew what true affection could be. Perhaps without that innate knowledge, I would never have been able to find Brian in the midst of the poverty that raised me. It was this thirst that had brought me my marriage and the boys who lay sleeping in their beds. It was this thirst that knew instinctively to keep photographs like the ones my mother had thrown away. Whether my mother had this thirst or whether she had learned, by some miraculous feat, to bury it, I understood that without it I could never save her. And she could never save me.

That morning Timmy came by early, and I watched him up on the ladder, a tool belt hanging from his hip. "Hold it steady," he called down to Keith and Chris, their combined eighty pounds pushed against the bottom step. He fitted the loose gutter back in its place and banged it a few times with a rubber hammer.

On the ground, he gave them a quarter each. "Hold on to that for ice cream," he said, and I watched him put a hand through his blonde hair, cut short before it could curl up, my mother's blue eyes smiling from his pale face.

"Let me take the boys this afternoon," he told me when he

sat down at the kitchen table. "We'll go to Adventureland."

I dropped four sugars and a dollop of milk into his tea. "Mom has to go." He made a movement with his eyes and I looked up in time to see my mother standing in the doorway.

"Fine," she said. I watched her take her Pall Malls off the counter. "I'll go." She headed for the porch. "I'm sorry," she said before she closed the door behind her.

"What's going on?" I waited until I was sure she couldn't hear me, and then I told him about the photographs. He paused with his cup mid-air. "Why?"

I shrugged, feeling the tears well up. "She thought they made me sad."

Out the window, a coat tossed over her nightgown, we watched her smoke. "I'm going to get her an apartment." I had stayed in bed that morning deciding what to do. I couldn't continue with college without my mother to help me with the boys, but I couldn't live with her any longer.

My mother stabbed her cigarette into the ashtray until sparks flew into the air. Timmy gave a quick shake of his head as if to clear the image. "I understand." He took a sip of his tea and put down the cup. "I'll take the boys today, give you a little time to sort this out."

After she closed the door to her room, the first phone call I made was to Gracie. With Matthew away at college, Gracie was on her own, and as I dialed her number I devised another plan. I told her the story I had told Timmy, and when I finished she was quiet.

"I can't imagine what made her do that, Kat, but you need to understand she was thinking of your best interests." I drummed my fingers against the kitchen counter to calm my nerves.

"I know, but she can't live here anymore. I'm taking her to look for an apartment, and if you'd like to, you can move in with her." I figured it would be good for all of us. My mother wouldn't be alone, and Gracie could help with the rent.

THE BRICK COMPLEX ON MAIN Street, just a few blocks from the house, showed signs of wear. There were a few flowers in window boxes where tenants made an effort, and a small a patch of grass. My mother walked quietly around the two-bedroom facing the street and when I stopped in front of her, she said, "This is fine." I took out my checkbook and paid for the first month.

The truck Danny showed up with looked like this might be its last mile. It was loaded with the tables and chairs and boxes my mother had stored for the last two years, and the remnants of Gracie's small house. With the help of Patrick and Timmy, my mother and Gracie moved into their own apartment.

Early Sunday, the bathroom mirror was fogged from her shower, and my mother was frying bacon and eggs in her new kitchen, fragments of her personality already decorating the apartment. On the dresser in the bedroom was the bowl Harry Banks had brought back from Denmark and would now forever be my mother's. In it were coins and movie-ticket stubs. Next to the bowl was a photograph of me with my arms around the boys, our smiles bright and shiny before they were made dull by loss. On the night table was her lifeline of prescription bottles, along with two packs of Pall Malls, and on the closet door, where most people would hang a mirror or a shoe rack, was her faded photograph of John F. Kennedy.

In the kitchen hung the potholder with a chef's hat, and on the table, her yellow tea cup the size of a bowl, and the glass ash tray that Danny once tried to kill Patrick with, already half filled with crushed butts.

Gracie's room held a double bed made smooth by her particular hands, a dresser with a lamp, and a clean ashtray. *It looks like a prison cell*, I thought, but kept that to myself.

"Grandma, we bought you bagels and cream cheese." Chris put the bags on the table and took out his cinnamon raisin.

"I thought I would help you unpack, but it looks like you and Gracie have been up all night."

She cut the bagel and smeared a thin layer of cream cheese

for Chris and popped Keith's in the toaster. "We were up late. Most of it is done. Not that I had a lot to unpack." She buttered Keith's bagel and cut it in fours the way he liked it.

"Tomorrow we'll go shopping. Pick out some new curtains," I said.

As we drove to Macy's, the boys strapped in the back, I asked her the question that had been on my mind ever since I found the empty photo albums.

"Did you really throw away all those photos?" I kept hoping that maybe she hid them somewhere.

Without turning to face me, she said, "I did. I'm sorry. Now I realize what I've done was wrong, and I can't undo it. I know you will never forgive me, but I want you to know I really did it for your own good. I hope you go on with your life and meet someone who will make you happy." Her voice was low and wispy, like a dandelion adrift in the breeze.

Since Brian's death I had come to trust in her love, put behind me the mother who never sat me on her lap, read a book to me, or came to my school plays. I tried not to think about feeling like a motherless child and thought she made up for her indifference by giving up her freedom and taking care of my sons, but now she had stolen my memories, something I could never replace. Brian, in his innocent death, had brought us pain, so she had rendered him invisible, plucking him out of our lives as though it were possible to find solace in that blank space.

THEY SAY TIME HEALS ALL wounds, and it occurred to me as the boys grew and I continued toward my college degree, that time was, indeed, a strange and often beautiful companion. It was comforting to know that it clocked on regardless of the tragedy or horror that humans brought forth. I learned this long ago from my mother's bachelor cousin, Delaney, and I thought of all those clocks, chiming in his apartment. Delaney was the only kind man in my childhood, and he had collected clocks. The combination of the two allowed me to understand the constant comfort of time advancing onward.

On Saturdays, Delaney rode the bus from Newark, New Jersey, to Penn Station, and then the subway to the South Bronx. Annie and I watched him walk down the street with a greasy bag of jelly donuts in his hand and a Brownie camera strapped around his neck, mumbling to himself. Though he was strange, we loved him because he took us to the zoo or the Botanical Gardens and bought us lunch, and because he was the weekend alternative to taking clothes stuffed in pillowcases to the laundry mat or washing the kitchen floor. He had no friends, no interests outside of playing the organ at Sunday mass. He never had a girlfriend, never had sex, and never drove a car.

We were his entertainment, his reason to put on a suit and tie and ride a bus and subway for four hours every Saturday. He took us to lunch at the Boulevard Diner where Annie ordered grilled cheese, I ordered a hamburger, and Delaney had tuna fish. Before we headed out, he would tell us we could invite a friend next time, if we wanted to, but Annie and I shook our heads in unison, picturing his chin, wet with mayonnaise, his tie stained with fish, his trousers doused with crumbs.

Sometimes, Annie and I ventured to his Newark apartment. It smelled the way old people's apartments tended to smell, moth-bally and stale, except that it was filled with clocks. And this had made it an enchanted, almost magical place. The clocks chimed and bonged and coo-cooed every half hour, reminding us that no matter what happened, time would clock on ceaselessly, an advancing constant.

When he died, Delaney left everything to Annie and me, including a clock that had been a hundred years old when he bought it, which sits on the mantel in my home. The clockmaker said it was a treasure, and I agreed. It is the showpiece of my living room, striking every half hour. During the years after the hijacking, it reminded me of how true it was that time healed. My children were adjusting, I was getting an education, and I was trying to forgive my mother.

The forgiving was gradual. It started with the reluctant acknowledgement that while I hated that those pictures of Brian were gone, I understood it was a desperate attempt to protect me. My mother surprised me by making it possible for me to go to class, taking the boys when I needed to study.

I understood too, when I looked at my boys running across the lawn, trying to goal a soccer ball, that mothers have their own lives—a fact a child cannot fathom. Sometimes in their grief and silence they cannot look their children in the eye. Sometimes they commit desperate acts to save them. And so my mother and I had a gradual coming together in those years, respectful, tentative, healing.

I had learned something else about time in the wake of the hijacking. It also dragged with it those things your mind could not erase. Time would not erase the bomb exploding in Rodman's Neck. It was still fresh and hot and terrifying in my mind. I still wanted answers to that question I had set a trial date to investigate: Why did the bomb explode? Was it rigged? Set to go off when the bomb squad approached? "We don't know," Charlie had told me each time I had pestered him for answers.

But someone did know, and when I thought of Julie Busic, tall and blonde, killing another woman's husband for a foreign cause, I had a sneaking, uneasy suspicion that the answer lay with her, and I would think of her in prison, killing time for that vicious, horrible crime.

...who at the best knows in the end the triumph of high achievement, and who at the worst, if he fails, at least fails while daring greatly...
— Theodore Roosevelt

What Then?

1978

I HAVE ALWAYS WONDERED IF, IN THE AFTERMATH OF grief, the universe balances out its harshness, and even those things that look like problems turn out to be gifts. I am not sure what happened next could have happened if my mother was still living with me. And perhaps my mother had opened some kind of space in that photo album, even if it wasn't her space to open.

It started on a hot day a few weeks after her move, when Timmy said, "Why don't you come to the Hamptons with Jean and me next weekend. Get out and meet some people." Jean and Timmy had been married for a year, a perfect match, we all thought.

"I don't think so," I answered. We were sitting at a picnic table in my Northport back yard watching Gracie play catch with the boys. She had settled into the apartment with my mother, but it was temporary, she told me, as she intended to marry Billy.

"I'm not ready to meet anyone." I didn't think the Hamptons was my scene anyway—swarms of rowdy people crammed into sweltering shacks, listening to music loud enough to burst your eardrums.

"Aw, come on," Timmy punched me lightly on the arm. "Beaches and outdoor bars," he said. "You'll love it."

"Go on, Kat," Gracie called. "Let Mom and me have some fun with the boys." And so I went on a weekend trip to the Hamptons with my brother and his wife that would change my life.

My overnight bag held shorts and tank tops and a toothbrush. Hot air blew through the rolled-down windows of Timmy's banged-up Chevy, and my hair whipped against my face. There was no AC, so we made do, and sang along to "You're The One That I Want." The kids and I had just seen the re-run of *Grease* at the old Northport Theater, and I knew all the words.

The day was heating up, and I began to regret not packing a bathing suit, but I lost fifteen pounds since becoming a widow and had not regained enough to fill in a flat chest and narrow hips, and there was my white skin that had not been exposed to the sun in two years.

Timmy pulled onto Dune Road and I watched waves crash against the dunes. On one side was the Atlantic, on the other, Peconic Bay, where houses with docks poked out of the sand. It was a million dollar view, but I was distracted by the thought of my mother letting the boys eat the bags of candy I knew she had stashed in her linen closet.

"The house isn't much, and there are four other renters," Jean called back. "But we don't spend a lot of time there. We usually stay at the beach all day and then listen to bands play under the stars."

A refrigerator and two threadbare couches filled the mud-colored living room. I opened the fridge and found it filled with beer, not an inch left for food. My feet stuck to the kitchen floor, which was big and bright and very yellow. "Why is the refrigerator in the living room?" I asked.

Timmy laughed. "Convenience."

Jean showed me to the room the three of us would share, where two single beds were separated by the length of my foot.

As I changed into shorts, I could see sun shining through the cinderblock walls.

The Cat Ballou was in full swing, a guitar player strumming to a song I had never heard, "Nibblin' on sponge cake, watchin' the sun bake; All of those tourists covered with oil." I seemed to be the only one who didn't know the words. Timmy parted the crowd and offered me a draft. "It's all they serve." His shrug was apologetic.

"It's fine." I clinked against their glasses. "This is great. Thanks."

We sipped our beers and looked around the open-air room, the Atlantic pounding against the shoreline. Bare bulbs had been strung over the raw wood dance floor where a barefoot girl in bikini top and cut-offs danced, and the rest of the room swayed along.

"Hey Mac," Jean called to a guy threading himself through the crowd of bathing suits. Mac squinted into the afternoon sun and gave Jean a quick kiss on the cheek, then extended his hand to Timmy.

"Mac Davis, this is Kathy, Timmy's sister." At first I thought it *was* Mac Davis, the country singer with the telltale dark, curly hair and magic blue eyes. But when he extended his hand, I saw this guy was younger.

"Jim Moran." His blue t-shirt matched his eyes, "but you can call me Mac." He grinned.

The place filled with beachgoers waiting in line for drafts, and we were pushed into a corner with a Space Invaders machine. Mac bet he could beat me. I didn't tell him I had two boys who regularly tried to take down my armies of aliens. Still, he won two out of three before he said, "Best of five buys dinner."

I gave it my best shot but came up short. "All right. I'll buy."

"No, no, just kidding." His eyes twinkled. "I would love to buy you dinner."

We made it a foursome, and Jean gave me a little hug on our way out of the Cat. "What do you think?"

I grabbed her arm, and we walked ahead. "He seems real nice."

She squeezed my shoulder. "I kinda thought you two would like each other," she said.

Indian Cove Restaurant jutted out on the Shinnecock Canal with a view of the marina and hundreds of sailboats. Mac and I fell into easy conversation about boats and Hampton Bays. He was a plumber, starting his own business, and I liked the way his hair fell onto his forehead, dark curls with a touch of gray, and those eyes, which made me think of Frank Sinatra. I told him about going back to school, that I was taking a photography class, how I had grown up in the Bronx. But I omitted the dreaded word widow, and the fact that I had two children, and kept feeling twinges of guilt. *Am I really laughing with another man?*

Jean was right. I did like him, his easy smile and dark good looks. By the end of the weekend, he invited Timmy, Jean, and me to a backyard party. His rental house was a palace compared to Timmy's. He was the only male among eight airline hostesses. They scrubbed the house and cooked for and doted over the easy-going guy who could fix anything. There was an ex named Kathy in that mix of women, but she didn't appear to mind my presence.

While we leaned against the railing, sharing a paper plate of shrimp, Jim asked, having just ended a relationship with a Kathy, "Can I call you Kathleen?" A name he said he always loved.

"Kathleen it is, if I can call you James."

In the next few months while my mother and Gracie invented things to do with the boys—a trolley ride up Northport's Main Street, a trip to the sweet shop, dinner at McDonalds—I hitched a ride to the Hamptons with Timmy and Jean.

James was more carefree than Brian, who had been a city kid like me. James was raised on Long Island. He rode his bike to the docks at Bay Shore, and his skin turned brown during summers of scraping barnacles and climbing sailboat masts.

He didn't have the cynicism that crept up on some policemen who saw the most debased of human nature. Brian had tried to hide that side, but he sometimes woke up in a sweat after bad dreams, and it showed in his eyes when he came home from a particularly gruesome scene.

The late summer day was brilliant with sunshine, and Hot Dog Beach was packed with sunbathers. James and I weaved around blankets and umbrellas. Humidity had turned my hair into a mass of curls, but I wasn't thinking about frizzy hair or a flat chest. The rhythm of the surf, the smell of lotion, and the strong man walking next to me erased everything but the moment.

We walked out to the barrier rocks across sparkling sand laced with star fish skeletons and watched a dad toss a lime-green Frisbee to a little boy who ran backward to make the catch. James took my hand to climb the rocks.

"How long until you graduate?" The stones were hot under my bare feet. The air smelled gloriously of summer, bright and shimmery. I lifted my face and felt the sun, hot and languorous, and sensed something special happening.

"Two more years."

His hand felt rough, a workingman's hand. A plumber wasn't who I thought I would date the second time around. I pictured a white-collar worker or an academic. But holding his hand was comfort, the weight of his fingers an anchor holding me down to the here and now, not what came before, or what might lie ahead.

"What then?" he asked. I didn't know what then, but I did know what now, and that was in the weekends we had spent together, James had taught me to laugh again. That was all I wanted right now, to hold a calloused hand, to let my hair fly in the wind, and to laugh with the man who looked like Mac Davis.

I WAS AFRAID TO INTRODUCE the boys to another man. I

didn't want to raise their hopes of a new dad, or worse, a man who would come in and then out of their lives. But at summer's end, when James asked to pick me up in Northport for dinner, I said yes.

My stomach did a little flip when he rang the doorbell of the house in Northport. Morty barked like a maniac while Chris chased him around the dining room. Keith was in the den playing the same keys of "Frere Jacques" over and over. My mother folded a towel and placed it in the laundry basket. From the threshold of the kitchen I watched as she raised her eyebrows, considering the man I brought home to meet my sons. I could tell she liked what she saw.

That night we sat at the Clam Shack and ordered soft shell crabs and a bottle of chardonnay, and I told him the story I had been avoiding for three months. It was always a cruel telling, no matter how the words were phrased, and I worried most that my terrible history might drive him away. Why would anyone want to get involved with a widow and two kids, especially one who had suffered such a disturbing loss?

His first question was about the boys and how they were taking Brian's death, and I felt my shoulders relax. I had expected him to ask about whether I was ready to date. And then we talked. We talked about death, what it meant, how mysterious and confounding it was, we talked about my mother helping with the boys and the boys themselves, who they were, what they loved, how they spent their time.

"I would like to take them for a ride in my new truck." As he told me about the truck, his schedule, when might be a good time, I tried to concentrate on what he was saying, but instead I watched the tendon in his neck pulse with life and imagined running my finger along its path, thought of his kiss, soft and sweet, pictured what it might be like to spend a weekend together. The idea of waking up next to James was both terrifying and exhilarating.

After dinner and a lingering kiss in the car, I told him I would make dinner for him the following week. He smiled. I didn't need to say the words. We both knew what that meant.

At my house, my mother sat at the dining room table where the piles of newspapers about Brian's death had been replaced by textbooks, and where she now had spread out the *Northport Observer*. I sat down in the chair across from her. "I would like to get to know him better," I said.

She stopped reading. She had a faraway look in her eyes. "Good," she said. "That will be good for you." More than anything, I knew she wanted me to have a second chance, something she never had, and that helped the memory fade of those missing photos.

Gracie babysat that Friday night. She was smoking a cigarette when James drove up, and her charm bracelets tinkled as she pulled the curtain aside to peek out at him. She whistled low.

"Wowee," she said. "He does look just like Mac Davis." She called up the stairs. "Boys." She winked at me. "We're leaving. Your mom has a date with destiny."

"Desperado," the Eagles sang, as I dressed a salad and James put a steak on the BBQ. After dinner we weren't awkward or hesitant. It felt like the most natural thing in the world when I took his hand and led him to the bedroom.

"I've wanted to feel you in my arms since the day I met you," he whispered in my ear. His white shirt smelled of clean laundry, his breath of after-dinner coffee.

I had forgotten what it was like to run my hand over the hard muscles of a man's chest. He was incredibly gentle as his fingers explored my naked skin. I thought about how wonderful it was to once again be touched—hot and electric—and let myself drift away from the last few years when I could not see beyond my sorrow. I explored the curve of his thigh and held on to the tenderness of his touch. When it was over, we were both breathless and smiling, my skin stinging in his absence. I could hear acorns falling from the tree outside my window, blown from the tree by the wind. Then the light patter of raindrops that became louder and stronger until the window was a sheet of rain.

IN THE MORNING JAMES MADE bacon and eggs, and we considered taking a bike ride but went back to bed instead, where we stayed until it was time for Gracie to drop off the boys.

The next weekend we took the boys to Skippers Restaurant, a walk up Main Street, ending at the harbor. It was our first outing together.

"I have a twenty-one foot Cabin Cruiser," James told them. "I hope you'll come out with me."

Chris let go of my hand and skipped next to him. "Can we fish?" James took his hand and they walked ahead.

"We'll catch lots of Snapper," James said, and Keith caught up.

"Can we try for Bass too?"

We walked out to the end of the dock and watched a fishing boat crawl across the sound, lobster traps stacked high, ready for their prey, its motor rattling the air. "Those are lobster traps," James told the boys. "Lobstermen mark their territory, and everyone knows not to pull someone else's traps." He had each boy by the hand, natural and easy.

"Do the lobsters bite the fisherman?" Keith wanted to know.

James leaned down to his level. "They wear protective gloves," he said. "And then put rubber bands around their claws so they can't bite."

Chris nodded. "I know. My friend's dog Max wears a muzzle so he doesn't bite anyone." He smiled at James, his eyes bright and sharp.

"Yes, exactly right," he said.

We ordered hamburgers, and Chris shook salt on his fries and then licked the top of the shaker before passing it along to James. James looked at me, his face a puzzle.

Embarrassed, I asked Chris, "Do you know you're not supposed to lick the salt shaker?" Chris lowered his eyes.

"Yes," he said, his face turning red. I tried not to laugh.

"But do you know *why* you shouldn't lick the salt shaker?" He looked up with a bright smile.

"Yes, because when the next person licks it he'll get my germs."

THAT FALL, JAMES DOCKED HIS powerboat in Northport Harbor where the boys threw nets for bait and fished for Blues. We went to Skippers once a week, he took them out in his truck, and when winter came, he taught them to ski. James was hardier than I thought, and stayed even after his family suggested he keep walking, told him that raising someone else's kids came with a shitload of trouble (his father), and he should find someone to have kids of his own (his mother).

I watched him teach the boys how to use carpenter tools, build furniture, fix plumbing. I loved the nearness of him. He felt so there, after the looming empty space Brian left in our lives. It had taken me a long time to imagine myself with someone else, but even in my most vivid imagination I could not have conjured up someone as understanding and sincere as James. I never thought I would find someone else who made me feel so special.

It helped that James looked different than Brian. He was taller, more muscular, his eyes a more vivid blue. "Frank Sinatra eyes," Gracie said. I knew he would never replace Brian, no one would, but he was charming, fun to be with, and I began to fall in love with this happy-go-lucky man and the risk he was willing to take with a widow and her ready-made family. It was a different kind of love. Brian, in his way, had saved me, had been my hero. But James was not saving me. I had been raising two boys alone, had gone back to school, figured out how to fight City Hall. I felt different stepping into this love—stronger, an equal.

In February, when the only tracks in the snow on Vista Drive were from James's F150, he unpacked his size large clothes into dresser drawers that once held mediums. He stacked his Jimmy Buffett cassettes on a shelf next to his shoes and sneakers and put on hangers his one suit and half dozen dress pants and shirts.

Snow blocked the sliding doors, and I stood watching Keith and Chris dig a tunnel, and Morty jump over drifts, puffs of white breath trailing into the frigid air. We had celebrated Keith's sixth birthday last month, and James had bought him a fishing pole that waited in the corner of his room.

"As soon as it gets warmer we'll go fishing together," James promised.

We took them to Disney that winter. Sunshine, after months of cold feet and slippery roads, was a perfect elixir. A half an hour after we arrived at the Lake Buena Vista Hilton in Orlando, James and the boys were in the pool, Keith on his back, Chris hanging from his neck.

I sat at the edge of the pool, my feet in the warm water. Chris swam over, water dripping into his eyes. "Can we call James 'Dad'?"

I wasn't surprised. While we were on the beach the first summer Brian was gone, Chris had asked a total stranger to be his dad.

"Why don't you ask him?"

He swam back to James and said loud enough for everyone in the pool to hear, "Mommy said we can call you Dad."

"I would like that." James splashed his two little boys, and they splashed him back, and all was right with the world.

When the sky was laced with pink and the boys tucked in, James and I sat on the balcony overlooking thousands of lights that illuminated the Disney village.

"Will you marry me?" It was the ending of a perfect day.

"Yes," I said, "I will marry you." The sun was just setting, a promising streak of purple.

*It's only after we've lost everything
that we're free to do anything.*
— Tyler Durden, *Fight Club*

Murray vs. The City of New York

While I had been discovering James, the trial had waited. Now, just when I was getting my life back together, it was upon me. In his wisdom, Phil DeCicco moved aside and suggested Thomas Stickel to represent me in the case against New York City. He didn't have the expertise Thomas could provide. "He's an Army man," Phil told me. "A criminal attorney who knows his way around explosives."

Thomas was different from Phil, like night is to day, and when I complained to Phil about his gruff manner, he said, "You don't have to like him. You just have to trust him."

Thomas Stickel had filed the papers without fanfare. And the *Daily News* had run a headline.

City: *It's Not Our Fault Bomb Squad Cop Died!*

"Bomb squad policeman Brian Murray, 27, who was killed September 11th trying to defuse a Croatian terrorist bomb, accepted danger as a 'risk of employment' and the city does not accept liability. It is manifest that the tragedy of the death of her husband in the course of his known extremely hazardous duty was a risk of employment. There is no suggestion beyond speculation that any negligence was involved."

"It's just a tactic," Thomas said. "They will say he accepted the danger of his job, and we will say they did not provide the equipment to keep him safe. We will make them turn over all the evidence from the explosion and then you will have answers."

When I walked from the parking lot to the Bronx County Courthouse, I passed young men waiting on street corners and remembered passing similar men as the subway sped by 161st Street on my way to Walton High School. I wondered then what they were waiting for. And I wondered again heading to court that day, seeing a similar group huddled together, smoking cigarettes, eyeing long legs in mini-skirts. Freezing cold, or blazing hot, year after passing year they were fixtures on the corners of New York.

The glistening steps and marble columns in front of the courthouse made the rest of the neighborhood look forgotten, tenement buildings marred by rusting fire escapes, sidewalks blackened with a million pieces of bubble gum. When I was a kid, I wanted to climb those steps and stand in the cool halls and listen in on cases where people were made to pay for their crimes. Now it was my turn to make someone take responsibility and learn the truth. And I was going to do it, I realized as I kept up my purposeful stride, no matter how much my childhood memory of Calvin Lin being bullied plagued me, or how afraid I was of alienating myself from the city I loved, the city that raised me.

Thomas was on the front steps waiting for me as I crossed the street that first morning. "Park in the Municipal lot," he warned me, "and do not wear jewelry or drive a flashy car. No mini-skirts." When I came up the steps, I saw he had a frown on his face, and I thought something bad had happened since our phone call the night before. But he said, "Your dress should have sleeves. I told you to dress conservatively." No good-morning, no how-are-you. I looked down at my navy dress that I thought was the picture of conservative, its knee-length longer than anything else I owned, a red belt softening the line. Without apology I fished the lightweight sweater from my purse, something I threw in at the last minute, although I guessed the courtrooms would not be air-conditioned against the summer heat. "Good," he said. "Let's go." I wondered if he was this gruff with all his clients.

"The judge." He nodded at a tall man with black-framed glasses who strode past us in the hallway without a second glance. "His name is Alfred Rosenblatt, on loan from Duchess County." A slow dread started in my stomach. We had hoped for a judge from the Bronx. I'd been there all of five minutes, and I was wearing the wrong clothes and had drawn a judge from out of town. I tried to think of something positive to change the shroud that seemed to hover around us, but couldn't think of a single thing.

I had pictured the courtroom like the one in *To Kill A Mockingbird*, and to my surprise, that is what it looked like. The Federal court for the Busics' trial had been sterile, an industrial room with tile floors, low ceilings, and rows of benches. The Bronx Supreme Court was a recreated movie set with marble floors and carvings around the ceiling. A gate ran along the front of the room, separating the judge and jury from the defense and prosecution, and rows of benches were assembled like a church with the judge at the altar.

As I followed Thomas to our table I looked around for Charlie but didn't see him. Glancing at the Corporation Council, I saw three attorneys deep in discussion. When they looked over, they made no pretense of trying to hide their contempt.

"Don't worry about them," Thomas tried to reassure me, but I was worried.

"Three against one," I murmured and wished for Gracie, but for only for a minute because I knew I couldn't sit beside someone whose life showed on her face.

"Come alone," Thomas told me. "The jury will scrutinize you, and we do not need to worry about what they will think about anyone else." He did not know Gracie, her habit or her history, but I knew better than to bring my sister.

When Thomas approached the jury that morning, his persona changed. He buttoned his suit jacket and stood to his full six-foot four. Dark and handsome, a lawyer who commanded the courtroom, he seemed to mesmerize the jury with his clear and forthright version of what happened on September 11, 1976.

"This case is based on two premises," Thomas told them. "One: the NYPD did not authorize specialized protective gear for the bomb squad, even though special equipment was available and employed by other departments around the world. There was a robot available, a remote-controlled vehicle outfitted with cameras, microphones, and sensors for chemical or biological agents, but they did not have this equipment. There were also special protection suits, flame and fragmentation-resistant, similar to bulletproof vests, which were not used."

Thomas paused and walked to the railing. "Brian Murray was forced to dismantle bombs with tools from his own toolbox, wearing street clothes." I pictured Brian standing before eight sticks of dynamite in a shirt and tie, a vest with Bomb Squad written on his back that couldn't save him. Thomas looked around the courtroom at the policemen in plain clothes. I followed his eyes and that's when I saw Charlie, who had entered unnoticed.

"Two," Thomas said, as though he had just said "one" a minute ago, "you will hear from Terry McTigue, Director of the International Association of Bomb Technicians and Investigators. As an expert who represents the most prestigious bomb squad in the world, McTigue ordered his men to approach the bomb without full knowledge of whether the bomb's wiring had been severed. Corporation Council will tell you that the bomb exploded without provocation, that the wires were severed and the device should have been rendered safe.

"In fact, when the men approached and attempted to remove the bomb blanket, somehow contact was made, causing the explosion."

Juror number four shook her head slightly as if to say, *what a shame this young police officer died because the department didn't protect him.* Thomas talked for another hour about the explosive device, and never once mentioned the Busics. The blame fell entirely on the shoulders of the City of New York.

Over the next few weeks, I made up stories about the six jurors, people culled from the same Bronx streets I knew as a child. Juror number one, a Hispanic man, lived in the South Bronx, probably close to Faile Street, and wished he were at his job rather than having to sit at a trial for this redheaded gringa. Number two, a bottle-blonde about my age, dangerously overweight, tried to like me but resented my slim hips and natural red coloring. Juror number three, a man in his sixties, squinted at me, the widow who was trying to worm money from the city. He would be hard to convince.

Number four, my favorite, and the one who would persuade all the others, was younger than my mother, Irish like me, with auburn curls that she set in rollers every night, and blue eyes that said, *I'm on your side.* Number five, young and handsome, looked sullen and bored. And juror number six was a black man in a shirt and tie who worked behind a desk and enjoyed the respite of the courtroom from the tedious paperwork that plagued his days.

It took four weeks for Thomas to lead the jury through the progress of the explosive device, from the time it was discovered in the subway locker in Grand Central Station, through the transport period, to the Rodman's Neck Firing Range where it was placed in a pit. He explained that the pit was a deep depression in the earth, and during a detonation, the men could climb out of it and take cover behind a wall of sandbags, which is what Terry McTigue, Hank Dworkin, and Brian Murray did.

He brought in military experts to dispute the theory that

the bomb exploded without provocation and presented a mock-up of the cast iron pressure cooker, which was crisscrossed with black tape that held the fake dynamite cylinders in place. Wires came from the bottom of the pot and extended outside it, where an ordinary switch was attached. He told the jury that McTigue's theory was that when the exposed wires were severed, the bomb would become safe to examine. But it had not been safe.

On our lunch breaks, Thomas and I sat in a small, stuffy room as he read from his notes and took big bites of an apple. I brought along a ham and cheese, chips, Snickers, and a can of Coke.

During the third week of the trial, Charlie took the stand. His face was broad and honest, and I willed him to look at me, willed him to remember that night he had come to my house and given me the idea to do just this: sue the city of New York, get the answers I needed so badly for my own sanity.

But he did not look at me. He answered Thomas's questions about coming on the bomb squad the same day as Brian, about his friend of six years and the hundreds of devices they worked on together. He nodded and looked at the back of the courtroom when he talked about how he and Brian were similar in nature and background, about the same age, both with military experience and munitions training in the Vietnam War. "You even looked similar," Thomas said, "the same coloring and build."

"Yes," Charlie answered, and lowered his chin so we couldn't see his eyes mist up. "We were friends." I heard he made sergeant, and in the years since I had seen him, he had aged in the way people do when their lives become more significant, a heavier weight on his shoulders, a hardness around his eyes.

You know what happened, I pleaded with him in my mind. *You're under oath. Tell us.* But I knew what he must be thinking, that if he testified the city was at fault, he would be back in uniform, or even in civilian clothes, looking for a job. He had his own future on the department to think about, the ladder he would eventually climb all the way to the commander of the bomb squad.

"You were part of the team of investigators who examined the evidence." Thomas raised his voice. "What conclusion did you come to about why the bomb exploded?"

Charlie didn't look at me. He turned his head toward the jury and said in a clear voice, "The cause of the blast was inconclusive."

I never spoke with Charlie Wells again, and he left the courtroom without saying goodbye.

THE NIGHT BEFORE McTIGUE TOOK the stand was a sleepless one. I lay awake next to James, watching the numbers on my digital radio tick off time. The last time I saw McTigue had been a few months after Brian's death. I had taken the boys to TWA Headquarters where the Flight Safety Foundation would present me with a plaque for Brian's sacrifice. But when I stepped into the elevator, there was McTigue, and for a startling moment, I could not help but stare at his piecemeal face. I had never gotten this close to him, and did not realize how damaged he was, one eye permanently pulled down, his cheek lumpy with layers of grafting. At first, he stared at me, and then he stepped forward so his back was facing us, and I watched the numbers rise.

"What's wrong with that man?" Keith asked.

"He had an accident," I told him.

McTigue must have heard, because his back stiffened, and he strode quickly off the elevator.

The room where the ceremony was held was small, and Captain Carey had been called up first, the pilot who had once applauded the Busics for their bravery and commitment. The room erupted in applause when his name was called.

Then McTigue and I were called up together. We stood side by side and accepted our identical plaques. I let him talk, and held onto the boys, wishing I were home reading them stories, watching cartoons, anywhere but here, next to the man who could not even look at me.

Later at the reception, I juggled Chris from one hip to another, not knowing who to talk to, when Congressman Mario Biaggi came up and offered his hand. "Mario Biaggi," he said. I watched him talk to McTigue, and I recognized the swarthy, gray-haired Irishman from the news. I knew he was an ex-cop.

He shook hands with the boys and then told me, "I am sponsoring a bill in congress that will give fifty thousand dollars to every police or firefighter in the nation who is killed in the line of duty. I'm going to see if I can get it pushed through for you."

I put Chris down and smoothed out my suit jacket. Fifty thousand was enough to buy a house, more money than I had ever imagined. Maybe this day had been worth it.

"I appreciate your efforts." He looked at me and smiled his politician's smile.

"I'll keep in touch, let you know." But when his office called again months later, it was to tell me that he did get the bill passed, but it would not be retroactive.

THE NEXT MORNING, AS McTIGUE took the witness stand, I felt myself drift into a place of cornered shame as he glared at me with what seemed like the same contempt he must have shown the Busics. His testimony was so convoluted and dogmatic that by the time he left the stand we were no closer to an answer than when we started.

My stomach tied in knots as I took the stand. My voice barely rose above a whisper when I talked about Brian, and I had to hold on to the seat to stop shaking. Hearing about the explosion that ended Brian's life made me feel as if it was happening all over again, and I felt torn apart. I spoke about his bravery, his plans for the future, our boys, how I wanted to know the truth of what happened that day. Every juror sat stock still, listening, and I thought of how far I had come since Charlie had first chosen not to answer my question.

Shaken and unsteady after my testimony, I stayed behind rather than join Thomas for his apple and water lunch. Sitting alone in the courtroom, waiting for our afternoon session to resume, I leaned forward and turned over the glossy photos lying on the table in front of Thomas's seat. And that's when I saw the photographs. At first I didn't know what I was looking at, a scene so gruesome that even the Fraunces Tavern photos paled in comparison. It was Brian, lying in a pool of blood, his jacket shredded, his face unrecognizable, his eyes wide open. This was what Charlie tried to protect me from, these pictures, so awful that they would forever haunt my dreams.

So this is it, I thought, worse than anything I could have imagined, the full measure of how it feels to lose a part of yourself, the part that makes your heart beat, the part that blossomed when Brian came into my life, the manifestation of the full measure of grief.

I watched myself as if I were stepping off a cliff. I don't remember how I drove home to Long Island that afternoon. I took Keith and Chris to my mother's apartment, knowing I couldn't look at my sons with those pictures in my head. I couldn't turn to James to comfort me from the pain of losing my first love, or even to Gracie, who I felt I was losing to Billy. I wanted my mother, and it saddened me to know that for most of my life we had never shared more than a roof and a meal, because now more than anything I needed her comfort, but she didn't know how to offer, and I didn't know how to ask, so I went home and crawled into bed and prayed for sleep.

On Monday morning, I arrived at the courthouse early. One Hundred Sixty-First Street smelled of cooking asphalt. White smoke lifted from the sun-soaked pavement still damp from a morning thunderstorm. As I walked up the steps, I kept seeing those photographs.

In his summation Thomas told the jury, "Every man on the bomb squad was a munitions expert. The blast was contained in the department's own demolition pit, and all the evidence was confined in a controlled environment. The world's finest forensic team investigated the case. The FBI investigated the case. With hundreds of experts and all the evidence, why was the cause inconclusive?"

Juror number four couldn't help but nod her head. Yes, you're right, she seemed to say. Why?

We waited. That afternoon, jurors filed in ceremoniously. They did not look at me. Even number four, who often gave me sympathetic smiles, did not turn my way. They looked tired, resigned. I thought about James and the hope that when the case was over I wouldn't have to think about that bomb exploding anymore, I could just love the man who had coaxed me back to life.

Judge Rosenblatt told us to take our seats. The courtroom seemed to be holding its breath. "I am reluctant to take this decision from the jury," he said. I could not breathe. "But there is no suggestion beyond speculation that negligence played a role in this tragedy. Officer Murray accepted danger as a risk of employment, and as such, the city is not liable. This case is dismissed."

The courtroom erupted. The three defense attorneys shook hands. Behind me I could hear other men congratulating them. I sat at the defense table, stunned. I turned to Thomas. "What does this mean?" He had seemed so sure of himself.

"It means that we lost," he said, snapping his briefcase closed.

He warned me there was no precedence for a police widow to sue the city, and this case would have paved the way for other police and firefighters to sue. I knew there was a possibility we could lose, but Thomas and I believed we had a strong case, and the verdict would have forced the City of New York to take another look at the protective gear that was now available. Now I was never going to know what happened.

I stood on the steps of the courthouse watching the old Bronx neighborhood, the subway speeding by, women sitting on stoops, a cop walking a beat. Before I walked to my car I noticed juror number four, who seemed to be waiting for me. I had nothing to lose anymore, and walked toward her.

"We would have voted in your favor," she said quietly as she reached for my hand. The long wait was over and I had lost, but the jury believed the city was culpable in Brian's death, and I felt validated.

At the still point, there the dance is.
— T.S. Eliot, *Four Quartets*

Skip the Church

WHAT I HAD DONE CAME TO ME SLOWLY OVER THE weeks and months following the trial. While I stayed up late reading books for school about Toni Cade Bambara's activism in Harlem, the suicide of Sylvia Plath, Doris Lessing's fight against apartheid, and the fate of Virginia Woolf as she walked into the water with her pockets full of stones, I realized I had, without meaning to, done something radical. Throughout history, women had been trying to find a voice. And even though I lost the lawsuit, I let my voice be heard, and broken a legacy of invisibility that had started long ago.

"Bill Hutchinson," I was told by the detective who answered the phone, "is not with the department any longer." He passed the call instead to Lieutenant Miller.

"You'll lose your pension," Lieutenant Miller said when I told him I wanted to remarry. Once again my hands felt tied by the NYPD. "Skip the church," he said quietly.

As children, my mother had seen to it we went to parochial school and made sure we attended Sunday Mass, so I knew she would not approve of a fake wedding.

Instead, I turned to Gracie, who helped me plan the day. I kept thinking of Gracie's short-lived marriage to Jacky, the bloody veil, the honeymoon with a stoned-out husband. That had never been my fate, but I carried a constant yearning for Gracie to find that high that comes from true, solid love. She functioned well as we made up the guest list and planned a simple reception. She was working nights as a barmaid in a small tavern near the apartment she now shared with my mother and Billy.

I was by her side a few months earlier when she stood next to Billy dressed in a light blue suit, said her vows in front of a justice of the peace, and then danced to Billy Joel's "I Love You Just The Way You Are." Then I held my breath to see what would come next.

Still, it was Gracie who designed the wedding invitations and helped me choose the off-white dress that hugged my body. She was the one to orchestrate the fib about getting married at City Hall, and the one who made the wedding cake with the slanty bride and groom on top, so that the day almost seemed like a bona-fide wedding.

There was no aisle to walk down, no "I dos" to speak, and I cannot remember the name of the venue overlooking Northport Harbor, which is now condos, but I do remember dancing with James, our friends and family toasting to our future, and Keith standing to tap a glass with his spoon and give his own toast. He had grown tall and thin like me, his hair a darker shade of red. The room was still as he gave a speech about his new dad: weekends on the boat in Northport harbor, rafting with his cousins, and about the night the wind had been blowing fifty miles an hour, and his dad stayed on the beach all night to make sure the anchor didn't come loose.

I danced with Chris, blonde and green-eyed, who loved to hold his new father's hand, hop into his truck for Saturday morning errands, and hand him tools as James measured and cut wood for a shed. Save for the familiar snap of old rage that came back when we had to tell our little white lie about city hall, the wedding was flawless.

I NOW TOOK SOLACE IN that rage. I learned from studying activist women writers in school that the injustices forced on women were often the kernel for community activism and great change. I found this out for myself at the New York City Line of Duty Widows' Christmas party that year. It took place at Harry's on the lower level of the Woolworth Building, an underrated structure on Broadway, so glorious it held lobby tours.

Once the trial was over, I never heard from the bomb squad again, but there were no repercussions from the NYPD. Commissioners moved on, replaced by new regimes, new faces, the trial forgotten, and so I stood at Harry's bar, ordered a glass of chardonnay, and felt at home. And that's when I saw the NYPDs newest widow, younger than I, striking, tall, and blonde. Her coat glistened from the cold. She stood at the door and looked nervously around, but made no move to walk into a crowd of women whose fate she shared. And then she began to cry.

When I walked over she took a tissue from her purse and blew her nose. "This is my first time," she said. "I thought maybe someone would be here to meet me." She dabbed at her eyes.

I knew about first times. My first time I had been shaking so badly I thought I was going to throw-up. I felt alone and in desperate need of someone to hold me up. The flash of remembrance was so acute, my eyes filled up, but I put a smile on my face so she wouldn't come unglued and looked for Phil Caruso, the PBA president. The room was so mobbed with widows and policemen I couldn't spot him.

"Kathleen Murray." I offered my hand.

She tried to smile. "Mary Beth O'Neill," she said. "I didn't want to come." She smiled a little now. "But my mother thought I should."

I nodded. I'd been through the same drill with my own mother. The other widows, who had been mostly my mother's age, had patted me on the back and asked how I was doing, hoping I would answer "fine" so they could move on.

Though I wasn't the welcoming committee she expected, I walked her to the bar so she could order a chardonnay. "Thank you so much," she said after her first sip, and we toasted a sad toast. The Emerald Society Pipe Band waltzed by playing "Amazing Grace," just like they had at our husbands' funerals, the dirges taking us back to a place we never wanted to go again. The noise in the room was deafening, everyone shouting to be heard, but I stayed with Mary Beth, feeling like a big sister.

"Is it your father who was killed?" she asked.

I let out a dry laugh. "I wish! Sorry." I glanced at her, but she didn't seem shocked. "If you knew my father you would know why I said that. No, my husband was killed seven years ago."

"You look so young." She took a sip of her chardonnay. "I think it's great that you've been able to make a new life. Right now I can't see past today, but I hope someday I will wake up and go about my day without this terrible ache."

I wanted to protect her from the truth: it had taken me many years before I could go about my day without missing Brian, even after I fell in love with another man, even after I found myself succeeding at school.

I squeezed her hand, "It will get better," I told her, and she smiled gratefully. I knew all the police widows, had felt their sadness, and Mary Beth's was no different, but I could see strength there, too, and I felt like she might be the person I had been looking for without even realizing it.

We met again a week later at the Oyster Bar under Grand Central, a place that still gave me the shivers when I thought of that bomb placed inside the locker. The cavernous room was permeated with a mild fish odor and noisy lunchtime conversation.

"The salmon is good. I used to eat here all the time when I worked on 40th," I told Mary Beth, and we both ordered a plate of it and talked through the afternoon like old friends about our families and our plans for the future. It could have been a snowy day or a sunshiny afternoon, and we would never have known it in this underground restaurant. Through the window, scores of people swarmed around the marble lobby, pulling luggage, rushing for trains.

"You'll lose your pension if you re-marry," I said after we had shared a piece of chocolate cake.

She was quiet for a moment. "That's not right."

"No," I said. "It isn't right. Do you want to help me change the laws?"

She stared at me a moment. "Damned straight."

I told her it was a state law, not city, not police. After James asked me to marry him, I had called Albany, written letters, but no one was listening. I raised my voice to talk over the din of silverware and dishes.

"If we rally other widows, get strength in numbers, we might be able to make changes."

She nodded. "I'll make an appointment for us to talk with my attorney, Jimmy Lysaght. His firm represents the PBA. He will help us out." Mary Beth had just hit upon the perfect solution. We needed someone with authority and contacts, someone who could offer legal advice, non-profit status.

"And I'll invite another new widow, Susan McCormack, to help organize," I told her. I had met Susan when the department gave Mets tickets to the widows. We both brought our boys, and mothers and sons became fast friends. "I think she might have some good ideas." We were changing the laws of the state of New York, and how strangely beautiful that it was the female literary masters who had given me permission.

JIMMY SAT ON THE CORNER of his desk, photos of him with Mickey Mantle and Ed Koch on the wall behind him. He was a big guy, Irish, fair-haired and ruddy complexioned. He thought starting a widows' group was a great idea, said he could help us with incorporation and not-for-profit documents, that we were welcome to use his conference room as our meeting place.

"And when you are ready," he told us. "I will get you a meeting with the governor, so you can plead your case."

"Survivors," Susan suggested when we settled into our new space. We had been toying with names.

"Something to do with police or shield," I said, attempting to draw a copy of a police shield.

Mary Beth looked at my poor drawing. "Survivors of the Shield," she said. "SOS."

We all laughed, the excitement building. We had a name, a place to meet, an attorney to help us with incorporation and not-for-profit documents, and a commitment from Jimmy that he would pave the way for a meeting with the governor of the State of New York.

On the drive home, the streets were crunchy with new snow, the air muffled against midtown traffic. I passed shoppers scrambling, laden with shopping bags, and thought about the struggle of police wives. Mary Beth and Susan couldn't make the Busics' time in prison any longer, and they couldn't tell me why that bomb exploded, but they were strong women, and they shared the willingness to do something revolutionary: turn pain into action, make the world better in the wake of violence. Women needed sisters. And as women we sometimes had to make our own sisterhoods.

My aim is to put down on paper what I see and what I feel in the best and simplest way.
— Ernest Hemingway

A Postmark from Prison

AFTER JAMES AND I WERE MARRIED, OUR HOUSE CAME alive. In the years I lived in Northport, the neighbors said hello but never invited me to parties or asked me to come over for a cup of coffee. But after James moved in, everyone knew my name and began to invite us to socialize.

"This is fun," I told Pat the first time she and Skip asked us to go sailing. I thought about the scene I had witnessed from my window the first Christmas after we moved in, when her husband carried her to the car, her mink coat glistening in the snow.

Now we were watching Skip and James tackle the jib. "I wonder why it took us so long to become friends?"

Pat laughed. "Try having a beautiful widow move in next door." This took me aback. I had never thought about it. "And," she said, "I thought you were running an escort service." I looked at her like she was crazy. "There were cars in your driveway every weekend, young men sometimes stayed overnight."

Now it was my turn to laugh. "Those are my brothers," I told her. "They stayed overnight to help me with the boys."

WITH JAMES AROUND, MY SCHOOLWORK got easier. I had a shoulder to cry on about a tough exam, he built me a darkroom in the basement for my photography classes, and listened as I painstakingly read my papers aloud because I caught mistakes better that way. Sundays, James bought bagels and made bacon and eggs. Then he would take the boys down to the dock to wash the boat and go fishing.

When winter came, I watched the boys on either side of him on the ski lift in Maine, their cheeks ruddy with cold, their ski pants covered in snow. They no longer had to be told to put their dishes in the sink, keep their rooms clean, finish homework, they did it all in anticipation of a weekend with their new dad. James wanted to adopt his two little boys, and I talked to Jimmy Lysaght about it. You're not legally married, he told me, and you would be required to change their name from Murray to Moran. I thought some day we would have that marriage certificate, but could not take away their name, as that would feel like I was erasing Brian from their lives.

We were happy, living a life I had never let myself imagine after Brian's death. Although the hijacking always hovered in the back of my mind, there were some days I forgot about it altogether. Until that Tuesday in April when it all came rushing back.

I HAD BEEN OUT RUNNING errands. As I turned the corner onto Vista Drive, I saw a squad car in our driveway. In Northport, Long Island, 45 miles from Manhattan, where the crime blotter in the Observer listed weekly offenses from drunk driving to an occasional B&E, where sailboats lined the harbor, and tourists bought ice cream at the Sweet Shop, a squad car in the driveway meant tragedy, accidents, a death. Two police officers stood waiting. The boys. I thought. Please, not my boys.

By the time I managed to park, my hands were shaking. The officer took off his hat and leaned into the window. I thought for a moment he was going to pull the keys from the ignition, cite me for some violation, and then I could laugh with relief. "Mrs. Murray?" He was so close I could see the indent his hat made on his forehead. I remembered the indent my father's fedora had made in the same place. "I'm Officer Silver." He hesitated. "Mr. Busic has escaped from prison. He has not yet been apprehended and we've been told he might show up here."

There was a moment of incomprehension, and then another when the fear that had bubbled up into my throat began to recede. My family was safe, the boys in school, James at work. And then the terror arrived as a sharp-edged memory. It was 4:00 a.m., the persistent ringing of the doorbell, red lights turning on our walls, a coffin lifted into the hearse in front of St. Agnes.

I hadn't thought of the Busics for a long time, not since the ten year anniversary. I pictured them walking out of prison together after a twenty-five to life sentence that guaranteed only ten. Only now I realized they hadn't been paroled.

The voice of the officer came back slowly "We don't believe Mr. Busic will try to harm you or your family, but as a precaution . . ."

Officer Silver was studying me. "Mrs. Murray? Are you okay?

I felt as though something had cracked inside and not yet broken. "Yes," I managed. *The boys are at school,* I told myself. "I'm fine." *James is at work. They're okay, everyone is okay.*

"Why don't you come inside the house?" Officer Silver opened my door. "For your safety," he added. The second officer had walked to our porch and was standing guard at the front door.

"State police have set up roadblocks and dispatched search teams from Orange and Rockland Counties," Silver said as we walked across our yard. "They're combing the area with blood-hounds." He sounded so official, as though every word was repeated verbatim from radio communication. "We doubt he'll get far, but you'll have a police presence around the clock until he is captured."

Both officers followed me into the house, putting in mind that dark uneven dawn years before, my mother washing my hair, Gracie in her stiff black dress, the three-volley salute into a hushed crowd.

Sunlight had moved past the window, leaving the kitchen in a wintery dusk. I found myself reaching for the keys I had just thrown on the table. "Actually, I'm going to get my boys from school, I want them with me." But the second officer interrupted me. "We have someone picking them up right now, Mrs. Murray." He was tall, square-jawed, a red head. His name tag read Sullivan. "Just a precaution."

The blue uniforms visibly altered the kitchen with their broad shoulders and gun belts, had slipped into the atmosphere and changed the air of the room where we had family meals. I tried not to let them see my hands shaking. I kept thinking of Brian in his uniform which still hung like a ghost in the back of my guest closet, along with my first wedding dress and some of Brian's things I never could bear to throw away.

While I made them coffee, Silver spoke in his deep Bronx accent, the short a's and long back chain shifts reminding me of my childhood. "From what we've been told, Mr. Busic shaved his head and face and made up a dummy with his mustache and beard." Silver took a sip of the coffee I gave him. His almost silent partner glared out the window as though daring Busic to walk down our street. "They believe he must have hidden in a crawl space," Silver went on. "And then lowered himself into the yard where he dug a hole under the fence. He wriggled through a barrier of razor wire." Silver touched his gun, a reflex I had seen in a lot of cops. "And ran away." My eyes went to the gun, a .38 like the one Brian had carried that lay in my night table drawer, minus the firing pin. "He is considered armed and dangerous." Silver set down his cup. "He'll be shot if he makes a move to harm anyone."

I thought back to the statement I gave to newspapers after the Busics were sentenced, how I had hoped for the death penalty, or life without parole. I remember telling a news reporter how disappointed I was with their abbreviated sentences, that ten years for killing a police officer was a travesty. Now I regretted speaking out. Would Busic come here to try to kill us?

Moments later I heard a car door slam and looked out to see yet another police car in front of the house. It was Keith and Chris. They both looked pale and frightened. I met them at the door.

"Busic escaped from prison," I said. "The police are here only as a precaution, to be sure he doesn't show up. He has no reason to cause us harm, but we have to stay inside until he is caught." I put my arms out toward Keith, but he turned and bolted up the stairs to his room and I let him go.

Keith lost his father in a violent death. He still had night terrors, woke up and didn't recognize me or his surroundings. He knew Zvonko Busic was the man who killed his father. Although I wasn't convinced that Busic would show up in Northport to kill us, his reaction said that he thought he would. A police officer had taken him out of school without explanation, drove him home in a squad car, another was parked in our driveway, and two officers stood in our kitchen. He had good reason to be afraid.

"There's nothing to worry about," I said to Chris and led him over to the couch. I put my arm around his shoulder. "This is just a precaution," I said, using Lieutenant Silver's words again. He shrugged out of my hold to face me. "I thought something happened to you. The police came to my school." Tears streamed down his face and he wiped them away, sniffling.

"I know, honey, I'm sorry. They're only doing their job. They want to make sure we're safe." Chris was on the cusp of independence, but today's unfolding took that away and he let me hold him for a few minutes until he calmed down.

I did not know where James was working, and had no way of contacting him. He sometimes came home for lunch if he worked in the neighborhood, and I didn't want him to come home to a mess of police cars in the driveway. He had come into our lives and smoothed out the wrinkles. The boys were his sons, called him Dad and looked up to the man who worked hard to make our lives easier.

James did not take Brian's place. Instead, he became my soft place, a respite from a darkness that threatened to engulf me and the boys. He taught me to love again, different from the innocent love I had for Brian. He accepted the constraints of my life as the wife of a dead hero and the long hours I worked on starting Survivors of the Shield.

When James did arrive home that afternoon, he took the news in stride, the way he did everything else. However, he refused to be held hostage, and argued he should be allowed to go back to work, something the police guarding our house couldn't prevent. "Busic doesn't know who I am," he reasoned with Officer Silver.

As I watched James's car pull away, I noticed small country birds line up on the overhead wires and marveled at their precision. The two policemen who brought Keith and Chris home from school talked quietly in the driveway, their presence enough to raise the heart rate of everyone who lived on this quiet street. They all knew my story, a young widow with two sons who later married a plumber. Our children went to school together, played together. They would want to know if a police presence concerned their safety and I wished I could tell them it didn't.

While we waited for Busic's capture I imagined him peering through the window, his grizzly face void of the beard that I remembered from his photos. I played out scene after scene of bullets flying, glass breaking, Northport police powerless to stop this terrorist who feared so little.

During our next two nights of seclusion, I slept little and watched as dawn brought into focus the oak tree outside our bedroom window. I dreamed that same haunting dream where I was searching my father's apartment in Bushwick, Brooklyn, which still smelled like cigarettes and grease, with the same stacks of paperback mysteries that served as tables for overflowing ashtrays. Room after room beckoned to me, Brian waiting behind each door, but instead of Brian's ruined face it was Busic's, pocked and menacing. "You cannot escape from me," he said in broken English. "I know where you live."

James went to work and I was alone with the children. The days stretched unbearably, with fits of temper from Keith, who tried to sneak out, and antics from Chris who stood at the top of the stairs firing grapes at us.

Finally, after two days and nights, they found him. He had been gone 30 hours, and was found sitting on the porch of a general store just miles from the prison, tired and freezing. The police officer who found him said he seemed meek, defying the wanted posters bearing his picture labeled armed and dangerous.

"I have a real problem," Busic told the officer. "I'm an escaped prisoner."

The officer said Busic told him he staged the escape because federal officials had reneged on promises of a parole hearing, and that his wife Julie had been denied parole eligibility for another five years.

After the police were finally gone, after the stifling presence of their squad cars and their vigilance had lifted, thoughts of the Busics lingered. Why were they denied parole? I wanted to close the chapter on this man, never again allow him into my life, but he did manage to unsettle me. *He knows where I live.*

I SHOULD NOT HAVE BEEN surprised when I got that first letter. Busic had escaped, adding five more years to his sentence. With Juile's denial of parole, that meant they both would be in prison for at least another five years, and this brought me some small satisfaction Still, there was some electric current running from the Busics to me, like a bomb ticking my name. I stood in my kitchen, sunlight weaving a patchwork on the floor, sorting through mail, when that postmark stopped me cold. *Federal Corrections Facility, Dublin, California. Busic, J.* Her handwriting was spidery, almost elegant. I could not bring myself to open it.

Instead, I put it in the junk drawer and slammed it shut, as if it might burn me.

While James and the kids ate dinner, I kept glancing at the drawer. Later, after bedtime kisses, I curled up on the sofa in my office and opened the sticky flap. *I would like to tell you my story,* Julie Busic wrote. *Enlighten you with the details of the hijacking.* The letter was single-spaced, the words crammed into the legal size pages as though she had too much to say and not enough room to say it.

Yes, I said to myself, moving to my cluttered desk and pushing aside my schoolwork to spread out the three pages. *I want to know. Tell me. And then I will tell you my story, so you may know the harm you've done.*

Her words surprised me. She wrote that she knew she had been the cause of so much unjust human suffering.

> *You are the one who has suffered most. How can saying how sorry I am ever be enough? Even the fact that I have languished in prison for so many years does not seem enough punishment for me.*

In the letter she swore that she would become a nun, that since my husband had been taken from me, she would do without hers as well. She would live because death would spare her the suffering she had inflicted on me. She said she was reminded every day what she had taken part in. Almost a whole page had been devoted to how good it felt to write to me.

I looked up from the letter. Time seemed to have slid into a strange never-land I could not fathom. The house was still, the boys and James were sleeping, assured that I was working hard on my schoolwork. Most of my evenings were spent here in my home office. I ran out of space on the shelves James built, and a small mountain of Toni Morrison's books were on the desk, Maya Angelou on the upholstered chair. Charlotte Perkins Gilman, Virginia Woolf, and Flannery O'Connor piled on the floor. They seemed to look on as I began to think about answering her letter.

Writing back to Julie may be a big mistake, I thought, but ultimately, who would better understand what I went through than the person who put me there in the first place? The temptation to write back to her was irresistible. *Say whatever you feel*, she wrote, and so I sat down at my old Selectric.

> Okay. You want to tell me what happened, go ahead. I'll listen. Then I'm going to tell you what happened to me because of your arrogance and misguided loyalty, and why I can't understand, since you were born in Oregon, you became a martyr for another country's independence and saw fit to encourage a scheme that endangered so many lives.

After that first sentence the rest came easy.

> I find it appealing to hear of your imprisonment. I make no pretense of forgiveness or condone your part in the crime, but I like the irony of our correspondence and the chance to write what I can't say to anyone else.

It was a relief, putting down what I had thought hundreds of times over the years. I wanted to make her suffer and could do it without recrimination. I felt some satisfaction in those words.

The next morning, I put that letter in the mailbox before I could change my mind. She had it coming to her, so why was I so nervous? The words she had written kept running through my head. I couldn't stop thinking about them. *Set things straight. Unload emotionally. I hope we will be friends.* Did she think writing to me would gain forgiveness?

The only person I told was Gracie, who raised her eyebrows knowingly, red lipstick imprinted on the cigarette between her fingers.

"Christ," she said. "What does the blonde bitch want, anyway?"

We look up at the same stars and
see such different things.
— George R. R. Martin, *A Storm of Swords*

My Secret

AND THAT'S HOW IT BEGAN WITH JULIE BUSIC. THE arrival of the postman took on a new significance as I imagined a letter in his bag, anticipated the truths she would reveal. What I remember most about those months and years was Julie's presence in them, how it somehow eclipses so much of what went on.

Truthfully, Brian's memory had begun to fade. I made myself believe I had dealt with his death, that I had finished mourning. I couldn't quite hear his laughter anymore, or remember the feel of his lips. The picture of him on the bookshelf in my office was one of the few that had survived my mother's efforts to cleanse him from my life. In the photo, he was wearing his police summer blues, standing in front of the fireplace at our neighbor John's house.

I had once mentioned to John that I didn't have any photographs of Brian, and he had enlarged and framed that one for me. Sitting at my desk writing to Julie about the hijacking made him feel real again. These letters brought him back to me. When I looked at the photograph, it no longer felt two-dimensional. I felt like he was beside me.

In some troubled way, I needed those letters to make sure he was not forgotten. Yes, I was remarried and loved James very much, but deep down the pain was still there. And now it felt as though that pain was something tangible, something I could put in Julie's lap, make her deal with it.

Often during those days, when I was driving the boys to sports practice or sitting at the dinner table with James, I found myself writing to Julie in my mind. *I can't imagine what it's been like to wake up in a prison cell every day, but I'll bet you thought about what your actions did to me and my children every single one of those days, and I'm glad. I hope you and your husband rot in prison. I hope you never see each other again.*

And she wrote back letters about how abusive, stark and lonely prison was and how much she deserved it.

> *It just seems too little that I have been in prison all this time. Yes, I have paid my debt to society, but I still owe you so much, I can't get this belief out of my mind, and there's nothing I can do, I can't bring Brian back, I can't repair the damage done to your sons. I feel so depressed sometimes that I can't even think about it. Yes, we have suffered, we have missed out on so much, perhaps I will never have the chance to have children, but still, I feel that it's not enough, that to really suffer what you have suffered, I would have to lose my husband, that's the only way I could go through what you have gone through.*

The revenge I felt was like a forbidden fruit I had not been able to taste until now. I told her how much my sons missed out on, not knowing their father. I told her of my own love for Brian, that he had been my hero in ways she couldn't even imagine.

I read her lamentations of how sorry she was, how horrible she felt about what she did to me, about the boys. She spilled forth as though she were trying to open her chest of drawers and show me everything about her life that lay inside. As the boys swam and sailed and played lacrosse and soccer, I thought about it. While I worked with Mary Beth and Susan on our plans for SOS, helping women widowed from similar tragedies, Julie was a presence. And every day I made sure I was the one who got the mail.

I devoured the letters at the kitchen table, first thing in the morning, or in the afternoons, right after I hurried to retrieve the mail. I read them curled up on the couch late at night. I asked her everything and consumed her life.

Why would you be with someone like that, anyway? I typed one night in the quiet of my study. How did you even meet him? Days later, the response came that she had met him in Austria. He had been poor, ill-dressed, not someone she would have picked for herself. But he had confidence. *And that confidence gave me confidence,* she wrote, *as though he could achieve anything . . . that tells you why I trusted him when it came to the bomb; it had always been that way.*

She told me she had had no friends when they were together, knew no Americans, he had been her sole source of comfort and support. While they were running from one country to another, she had been dependent on him for everything and surrendered to all his goals because they felt noble, and worthier than hers, though she admitted she wasn't sure what hers were. *When I read his letters to me now, I get so frustrated . . . it seems like he thinks nothing has changed, that I am still his disciple in a way.* It sounded from her letters like Busic had hypnotized her, taken her as a kind of prisoner, seduced her into doing his bidding. I had no idea, as I devoured her words, that perhaps she was doing the same to me.

In one letter I braved the question I had wanted to know the answer to for so long. *Why did that bomb really explode?* Just days later, when I checked the mail, Julie's follow-up letter was there among the catalogues and bills. I kept it hidden in my first bureau drawer. The next day after I sent the kids off to school and kissed James goodbye, I slipped it out from where it lay between my lingerie and slips.

Zvonko would never hurt an innocent person, he took

every precaution to ensure that the bomb could never go off accidentally, so when he heard what happened, his first thought was of sabotage, that the Yugoslavs had heard about the bomb and had set it off remotely as the police officers approached it. He was so certain it had been detonated purposely to discredit us, and Croatians in general. He will never understand how it could possibly have gone off.

When I looked up, a slanted gray rain had started outside, and I felt the expectation I had about knowing the truth sink like a cannonball. I had already heard this sabotage theory; it had floated through the media. I knew it was ridiculous. How could the bomb be accessible to Yugoslav extremists? From the time it was taken from the locker until the time it exploded, it was in Brian's hands. Why not detonate while it was at Grand Central, where it could do the most damage?

I looked back down at the letter.

I never approved of Zvonko's plans, she wrote. *I never thought it was right; I tried to dissuade him and failed.*

But you stayed with him, I wanted to scream at her. You were by his side.

What I would come to know about Julie was that she could anticipate my penchant for finding the truth. From 2,500 miles away, she knew how to answer it. In the next line she wrote:

I felt I had a duty to stand by him, come what may, because I believed, as he did, that he would soon be killed by the Yugoslav secret police, and he wanted to make one desperate attempt to bring the Croatian situation to the public before he was killed . . . many of his friends and relatives had already been murdered in Europe for their political views, and he was told by many that he was on the top of their list as well. He thought if he could get the truth to the public that our government could bring pressure on the Yugoslavs. I was in the position of not knowing what else he could possibly do, other than such a desperate act, and I therefore chose to be at his side.

The phone on the bedside table rang, but I ignored it and kept reading.

I also felt that I could be a calming influence on everybody on the plane, that I could help maintain a calm atmosphere, which I did. But I never condoned it, never believed it was right. I just didn't know what else could be done to maintain my husband's safety. The situation was just an impossible one.

And how ridiculous for the police to warn you when Zvonko escaped, as though he would want to harm you for any reason, had picked your family out and was intent on preying on all the members until there were no more.

She made everything seem so reasonable. She was so pragmatic. And yet some warning bell went off inside me: Was this compelling woman my ally or horribly disturbed?

Still, I answered this letter, and I waited for the next. The synergistic ways our lives merged, the odd coincidences were, in some way I didn't want to look at, titillating.

IN THE LATE 60s WHEN Julie began her new life in Vienna with this depraved, terrifying man, Brian and I had been planning our future. We were twenty-one and intended to wait a few years before we married so we could save money, prepare for a family. But driving home from the Bronx to Brooklyn one night, he fell asleep at the wheel, drove his Volkswagen into a guardrail and was taken away by ambulance with a concussion and broken ribs. We were married three months later.

In 1970, eight bomb blasts rocked New York City within a

few months. A revolutionary group, The Weather Underground, declared war on the United States Government. Their weapon: bombs. The New York City bomb squad could not keep up with the multitude of cases, and two young men were recruited from the rank and file of the police department, Brian Murray and Charlie Wells, both military munitions men.

In another underground operation in Vienna, a group of Croatians declared a war of their own. They would no longer stay silent while the Yugoslav government persecuted their families. Julie went along with Busic to these covert meetings.

Busic had been expelled from his homeland for having plotted to start a civil war and was in Vienna on a work visa. He had a mission: tell the world about the atrocities the Serbs perpetrated against the Croats. In her letters, Julie repeated again and again how much the radical ideas thrilled her. She wanted them to be co-conspirators, make a difference. It didn't matter that Croatia was a country she had never visited, didn't speak the language and knew little about its government. Being with Busic gave her the significance she craved. She found herself constantly acquiescing to his power, one higher and more dignified than hers, one she could not resist, until she was no longer Julie Schultz from Gearhart, but the lover of a political radical, infamous in his country.

Anxious to prove herself worthy of her new lover, she flew to Croatia after Busic assured her that as an American, she could enter the country as a visitor and discreetly drop flyers from Zagreb's only skyscraper. The flyers were in Croatian, signed by Croatian Revolutionary Youth, and called for an uprising against President Tito who, Busic told her, had taken their language and their freedom. Julie admitted that she did not know the author, nor the full impact the dissemination of the information would have on the citizens of Zagreb, but she accepted this mission as a sufferer for their cause.

I pictured a young blonde, backpack filled with anti-government literature, stepping up to the parapet and sending reams of paper cartwheeling to the ground while passersby cheered the message. I imagined Julie's exhilaration, her flushed cheeks and rapid heartbeat at having been the source of the chaos.

Busic told her she would be able to slip out of the country unnoticed after the deed was done, but instead she was thrown in prison and shared a cell with gypsies and whores, a hole in the ground for a toilet.

Why didn't she leave Busic after she had gotten out of the Yugoslav prison? I asked. She wrote back that she had fallen deeply in love. She said that if Brian had been in the IRA, she believed I would have followed him for similar reasons. *Of course, neither of us today would do any such thing,* she said. *But years ago Zvonko's love was just too important to me. I could not bear to lose it.*

I wrote her back that I understood the need for change in nations where citizens were oppressed and agreed with much of it, but I had two children, went to work every day, and had been married to a man who had volunteered to fight for his country. We went to church and prayed for peace.

"GRACIE, LISTEN TO THIS." JAMES and the boys were at a Yankees game. Gracie was on the sofa doing her nails while I read the most recent letter. "Julie's been in prison before."

"I'm not surprised." She blew on her nails. "Anyone crazy enough to hijack a plane," she said, "isn't afraid of prison."

I sat back in the chair. Outside the breeze had picked up, and in the half-light of dusk, I saw the sheets I had pinned on the line billowing like sails. Gracie spent eighteen months in the Bedford Hills Correctional Facility. I remembered waiting for her letters, the script a map to her life there. Because she was soft-spoken, freckled face, red haired, and slight, she had been targeted by prisoners and guards alike and had written she was terrified for her life.

When I turned, she was watching me, crows-feet noticeable around her blue eyes, a smattering of freckles visible against her pale skin. Her hair fell around her shoulders, wavy in the place that had held a ponytail.

"Someone slashed my arm with a shank while I was in line for dinner." She said it so quietly, I almost couldn't hear. "At first, it didn't hurt. I didn't even know I had been cut until I felt something wet, and then it burned like a blow torch."

I watched her shake her head, as though dismissing the memory. She put the brush back into the bottle and screwed on the cap. "They took me to the infirmary and stitched me up and sent me back to my room," she said quickly. "I never found out who did it." Tapping out a cigarette, she held it between two fingers, carefully reaching for her Bic so as not to smudge her polish.

I tried to see her scar, but her cotton blouse covered it. "I thought that scar was from the hit and run."

"Don't tell Mom," she said. "She thinks it was the hit and run, too."

That was the way with Gracie. I thought I knew everything about her, but I was always understanding there was more. She was labyrinth-like, a maze of known and unknown stories. I closed my eyes. Julie's last letter seemed to settle in my mind like one of the sheets on the line, settling after a breeze. Suddenly Julie and Gracie seemed to fuse, twin-like in my mind. I wondered vaguely about the ways we allow certain people to fill the spaces in our lives. Gracie blew out a stream of smoke.

"You know what prison does?" she asked. And when I didn't answer she said, "Prison makes you strong."

*She was becoming herself and daily casting aside
that fictitious self which we assume like a garment
with which to appear before the world.*
— Kate Chopin, *The Awakening*

The Doctoral Student
from Faile Street

ON A BEAUTIFUL SPRING WEEKEND, THE SAME WEEKEND Chris received his first Communion, I received my tassel—gold—not the black that adorned hundreds of others. "Magna cum laude," I shouted to James, so that everyone within a quarter mile could hear.

"I'm so, so proud of you." James twirled me around, sending my hat flying. The boys didn't know what magna cum laude meant, but James did, but they laughed along with us.

We gathered at the house—the Martins, the Murrays, and the Morans—so many we spilled into the backyard next door. My mother posed with me for a photograph in my cap and gown. Her red hair had been done at the beauty parlor, and she had on her pretty green dress.

"This is my degree too," she said.

"I know it is." I kissed her cheek and felt a special tenderness toward her. She had made it easy for me to hole up in my office and study for exams, brought over trays of macaroni and cheese and chaperoned dozens of sleepovers while James and I migrated our first years of fake marriage into a new decade.

Gracie and I posed for pictures and ate barbecue. I saw my mother laughing with Aunt Delia and watched Brian's brother Dennis set up a Whiffle ball game for Keith and Chris. Dennis was more square-jawed and bigger framed than Brian, and I saw something of him in Chris. He was an FBI agent, a man used to taking charge, but he was here today for us.

"Congratulations," he said when he hugged me, his voice so similar to Brian's it took me back in time. "What now?" he asked, and I laughed and told him I had just graduated, now I needed some time to decide.

"What now" was the same question James asked that day on Hot Dog Beach. Now I had a bachelor's degree in my hand, I could pursue a writing career, but something held me back. The boys had adapted to James, but they were still vulnerable, the way kids are who have lost a parent and gained a new one. I wanted to stay as close as I could to them. And then, standing there watching my youngest son on home base, ready to hit, I realized what I had wanted since I was a ginger-haired girl in a kindergarten classroom in borrowed clothes.

The house was filled with everyone I loved, and it was James I sought out to tell the news. "I've decided," I told him when I found him filling the ice bucket in the kitchen. "I want to be an English professor. I'm going to apply for the doctoral program." James took me in his arms and kissed my forehead. "You can do anything you put your mind to Kathleen, I have no doubt about it."

"SEVENTEEN APPLICANTS WILL BE CHOSEN out of hundreds who have applied," the Dean of Graduate Programs told me during my interview. It seemed a long shot.

I filled out the applications and read over the course catalogues spread out on the dining room table. Next to them was Julie's most recent letter. She was the one who had been born with all the opportunities. I was the kid from the Bronx who loved to read. Then, with the acceptance letter in my hand,

I planned out the next four years when I would receive my doctorate degree.

WE BOUGHT MY MOTHER a small house in Northport that she shared with Gracie and Billy. She was happy to be close to the boys, and I was happy to have help as I began my journey toward my last year in the program. But while I was teaching one afternoon, I found myself overcome with dizziness.

After collapsing in a chair in the office I shared with Jenny, another doctoral candidate, she looked at me in alarm. "What's the matter?"

"Can you take my class?" I asked her. "I'm sick." Putting my head down on the desk, I closed my eyes.

A while later Jenny brought back my purse and books. "The flu?" She put her hand on my forehead, motherly concern in her eyes.

"You don't feel hot. Maybe you're pregnant."

"Don't be ridiculous. I can't be pregnant." But then I remembered buying a box of Tampax that month and, without a thought, adding it to a full box still on the shelf.

"Oh God. You might be right."

Could I have gone two months without noticing? The panic came back. I knew she was right. My breasts had been sore, but I had not thought much of it. James and I did want a child together, but after trying for years, we decided it wasn't meant to be, and I went on with the PhD program.

It was late afternoon on a warm day in May. The kitchen smelled of the rich coffee James was brewing. When I told him about the baby, his hug knocked the breath out of me, and as he let me go I saw tears brimming in his eyes. We couldn't stop smiling at each other.

"You're going to have a new baby brother or sister," James told the boys after we had called them into the room. Keith's scarlet face told us he knew where babies came from, and Chris yelled, "I want a sister this time."

While the boys went back to their video games we sat on the couch, held hands, and smiled. And then we made plans for how I would have a baby and complete my doctorate.

"It will work out fine," James told me. I hoped he was right.

WE WERE AT TIMMY AND Jean's for a Halloween party, dressed in roaring-twenties garb. We had just asked them to be godparents when my water broke. The ambulance rushed me to the ER where our daughter was born early. Kaitlin Jean Moran weighed in at four pounds five ounces. At home, she took two ounces at a time, and I spent most of the day feeding and changing her, and realized how much special care a premature baby would need.

I would have to withdraw from the doctoral program, but would leave Stony Brook University with a Masters degree. It was still something to be proud of, I knew, and I thought about that time so long ago when I had shared a tiny room in a Bronx tenement with Gracie. Back then I had little chance of higher education, but by some miracle, I had succeeded.

The eyes of others our prisons;
their thoughts our cages.
— Virginia Woolf

Gravitational Pull

THE CALL CAME IN THE MIDDLE OF THE NIGHT, AS MOST bad news does.

"The ambulance just took Mom to the hospital," Gracie said. "I'll meet you there."

I woke Keith to tell him to listen for Kaitlin, that we were leaving for the hospital where his grandmother was, and then James and I dressed and tiptoed from the sleeping house and drove to the hospital.

"She had a massive heart attack," the doctor told us. "And considering the damage already done to her heart by her previous attacks, her heart is significantly weakened."

Gracie and I sat by her side in the emergency room. When the rest of the family had all gathered around her, she opened her eyes and smiled a tight smile.

"Looks like I'm not ready yet," she said, like she was in control.

"She is right," Dr. Balzac told me when I spoke to him in the hallway. He was an elderly man with half glasses perched on the end of his nose and a slight accent I couldn't place. "But the damage has been done," he said, as he stared past me into her room. "She will be on medication that can cause excessive bleeding, and she will need to be cared for by professionals." He removed his glasses and looked at me out of grey-green eyes. "Blood is no longer circulating properly to her legs. She will never walk again."

Never, I realized as I sat with her, feeding her canned peaches from her hospital tray, never get to live out her life in the house she had come to love.

She was transferred to St. James Nursing Home where we played checkers and listened to Frank Sinatra sing about New York. One morning I wheeled her chair outside so she could feel the warmth of the sun. But when the chair hit a blip in the sidewalk, my hands left the grip, and she began rolling into the street.

"Let me go," she said to me when I caught the chair.

"But Mom," I said. "I have you." She waved me away.

"Let me die," she whispered.

That afternoon I watched her sleep. A part of her had withered away, her face now drawn and wrinkled. After all those years feeling that I was a child without a mother, I finally had her in my life. I had given up the resentment and accepted a new kind of love she offered, and now I would lose her. It seemed, sitting by her side, that time was the worst thief.

I STOOD IN CHURCH ON Sunday, singing hymns next to James and my children, thinking about my mother. She had been the first family member there after Brian's death. She had picked me up during those horrible post-death days, found me things to wear, taken care of the boys, and finally come to live with us. Whatever faults my mother had, when the worst crisis hit, she had appeared. And now I realized her objection to Julie Busic was a sound one. I could see the folly of writing to the person who had turned my family's life upside down. She was an accomplice to killing the father of my two innocent boys and had threatened a nation.

I knew it made no sense, but my appetite for Julie's letters and their intensity felt almost sexual in nature. She wrote like a lover, crawling back to me, and sometimes I found I had memorized lines of her letters without meaning to, as though they were actual conversations, stamped into the mind's eye.

> *I still agonize over what you have been through, I still feel that I must do something to atone, I must help you in some way, but how can I do this? So much I know now that I didn't know then. But it's just too late now. At least I have become wiser with the years. I have not remained stuck in the past.*

We got up to file out of the church. I said hello to our priest, and ushered Kaitlin and the boys into the blaring sunshine, and felt the secret of those letters, the weight of them, moving with me. I realized as I climbed into the hot car, James behind the wheel, with the kids buckled into their seatbelts, that the letters threatened to send me back to a time when I couldn't see the sunlight but felt powerless to stop. I knew she was toxic, and I did not care. I was drawn to her the way I was drawn to the wayward girls in my South Bronx neighborhood when I was a teenager. I was drawn to her in the same way I had been drawn to Gracie, even while she was using.

The letters had a gravitational pull to them, as though they were alive, and I often stayed up until after midnight reading and replying. That night I slipped in bed next to James. The moon was high outside the bedroom window, and I could just make him out, his tousled hair, the sweet way his mouth opened slightly when he slept. I wanted to wake him and tell him. It had been two years, and I didn't want to keep the secret anymore. Sliding between his arms, I felt his big hands around my waist. He worked every day to support our family, and not telling him felt like living a double life.

I closed my eyes and remembered that he told me early on in our relationship that the details of my marriage to Brian and all that came with it troubled him, and he preferred living in the present. He once had a dream where he walked into the living room and found Brian dressed in a suit of armor. When James asked him what he was doing, Brian said he was waiting for me.

And so we built our own foundation. My life with James was what I longed for since losing Brian. I had someone to love and take care of me. I had three healthy children, an excellent education, great friends, and a beautiful home. But I also had a secret that I knew would hurt him if he found out and decided I would not tell him.

But while I lay there in the dark next to him, I knew, too, that something was missing, some part of that child I had been, who wanted to know what heroin felt like but was too afraid to try, the one who surreptitiously admired a monstrous brother with a voice like an angel when he rhapsodized crowds on street corners, the child who loved to roller-skate on Bronx streets in the middle of the night and was secretly thrilled when police raided Calvin's Chinese Laundry. That girl was pulled toward Julie's letters in the same way many of us are pulled toward the illicit. I realized that the illicit held a familiar charge. It was part of my DNA. Like a child raised on certain foods who then longs for them throughout her adult life, a part of me longed for something dangerous, something that felt like a brush with fire when you did not quite understand you'd been cold.

Drifting off to sleep, my hand over James's, I felt the comforting familiarity of the wedding ring on his left hand, but shame washed over me. Keeping Julie's letters secret reminded me of how I felt about the black eye and the broken hand Corky had given me, it was equal to trying to hide that my favorite older sister had used heroin. It was equal to the feeling that maybe I would really never be better than that kid who got sent home from school with borrowed school clothes and lice in her hair.

"I wonder what Julie thinks about me," I said to Gracie the next afternoon when the boys were at school, and she had come by for lunch.

"She probably wishes she never heard your name, but I don't think she spends too much time thinking about you."

"I'll bet she would be surprised at how much time I spend thinking about her."

Gracie took a sip of her Coke. She had not touched the sandwich I made her. And then she said suddenly, "I'm moving to Florida. Billy wants to go down there to fish."

Billy: vodka, cigarettes, stained yellow teeth, fingertips brown from filter-less Chesterfields.

"Florida's for old people," I said shakily. "People go there to die."

"Clearwater," she said, as if I had not spoken. "We're leaving in a month." I watched her pull out a Lucky and push her sandwich away.

I turned silences and nights into words.
What was unutterable, I wrote down.
I made the whirling world stand still.
— Arthur Rimbaud, *A Season in Hell*

Red Flag

WHEN GRACIE FIRST MOVED TO FLORIDA WE TALKED almost every day, about the weather, the flamingos and seawater sunsets, my mother's static health condition, the restaurants in the old city and how the humid air smelled of salt. I tried to tell her about Julie, but Gracie got very quiet when I did, and yet I couldn't help myself. Gracie was still the only person I confided in. She was my only outlet for the pressure of keeping the communication cloistered. I told her that Julie wrote about some of the passengers who went to visit her in prison.

"They said they appreciated life more now that they've learned the difference between what is trivial and what is important," I read from Julie's letter.

On Gracie's end I heard the lighter spark, the inhale of smoke.

"They were glad they had the experience, as it caused them to think about the things in their lives they wouldn't have explored otherwise."

Gracie was quiet. I heard her breathing. Finally she said. "You think that's true?"

I did not know whether she was asking if the passengers really came to visit her or if the passengers themselves appreciated being hijacked.

"I don't know," I said doubtfully.

"Well," Gracie inhaled. "Hijacking is trauma." She was quiet for a minute.

"And trauma is hell, no matter how you slice it."

And then she abruptly changed the subject. She talked about her cat and the dress she wanted to buy, and I let my attention slide from my sister to the last letter I had received. Julie wrote that Patty Hearst was in the same prison and had relayed to Julie what it felt like to be kidnapped and then to go along with her captors.

> *I have, of course, had many different kinds of experiences here over the years, met lots of interesting people. Sara Jane Moore is here now, Ma Anand Sheela, the Bhagwan follower. We've had a wide assortment of characters, gangsters, public officials, Russian spies; you name it, they've been here.*

I wanted to tell Gracie that Julie had been beaten with a hammer by Squeaky Fromme, the nut-job who tried to kill President Ford, but I saw the tables had ever so slightly turned, and now it was Gracie who was looking down at my wayward behavior, wondering when I would fly straight again.

I CHOSE TO IGNORE THE first red flag that showed Julie's true colors. The warning call came from an odd source: McTigue. In a strangely intimate gesture, Julie had begun to send me excerpts from her journal, and in it she described McTigue:

> *His face is a Dali or a Picasso face, off-center, the angles all wrong. Nothing matches up, one side sags, the other looks as though the skin has been stretched over a bumpy canvas.*

She complained that McTigue appeared at their parole board hearings and that thanks to him they had not gotten what she termed more favorable release dates. On one occasion, McTigue told the parole board that he was appearing on my behalf. She wrote that these appearances were damaging for her and Zvonko, that the parole examiners put a lot of weight on his statements.

In the next letter, I found folded up in fours, a copy of McTigue's letter to the Department of Justice, where he called her an "attractive and sympathetic" witness who was basically playing dumb. In it, he made a case for keeping her in prison, stating that if what Julie claimed in court was true then:

```
She did not know the purpose of the several cast
iron pots, packages of silly putty, wire, tape,
and material purchased to manufacture the simu-
lated and actual bombs.

She did not know why her husband wired together
sticks of silly putty, wire, batteries, etc. to
form a body harness that was ultimately used to
intimidate the passengers of flight 355.

She was unaware that her husband had purchased
TWA airline tickets under false names.

She did not know that her husband had checked
out flight 355 on Monday evening, September 6,
1976, and purchased one of the tickets while at
the airport.

She did not know that her husband possessed
60,000 leaflets dealing with an indepen-
dent Croatia that he wanted to drop from the
skyjacked aircraft while over France and Yugo-
slavia.

She did not know of the note to the pilot
demanding control of the aircraft, the multi-
page political diatribe left in the locker for
eventual publication in the world's print media
and the extortion note left in the locker—all
```

```
typed in the apartment on a borrowed typewriter.

She must not have known of the existence of
eight sticks of dynamite, electric blasting
caps, a large battery, wire, rolls of black
tape, switches, and other bomb making parapher-
nalia that Zvonko Busic admits having in their
apartment. And deteriorated dynamite gives off
a sweet odor that causes headaches and that the
nitroglycerin leaking from the cartridge forms
beads that permeate and leak into adjacent
areas.
```

He reminded the parole board that she was part of a carefully crafted air piracy plan to jeopardize the lives of tens of
thousands of innocent travelers. He urged them to set the
longest possible date for parole and send a clear message that
```
sorrow after the act does not qualify the terrorist
for leniency or special treatment.
```
Just so you know what kind of sadistic man he really is, Julie
ended her letter. But I did not think the letter showed a sadistic
nature. I thought McTigue, of whom I was very disappointed,
had a persuasive and rational argument.

It should not have surprised me, then, that the next letter
asked if I would consider writing a letter on Zvonko's behalf.

> *It would be the most important letter he could have,*
> *if only to counteract the lies McTigue told regarding your*
> *support of his efforts against us. Because I love him and*
> *worry about him if he has to spend more years in prison, I*
> *naturally would consider a letter from you the biggest help*
> *he could possibly have. You've been so generous and kind to*
> *me, and I won't ever forget it. It would've been really easy*
> *to be vindictive and vengeful.*

I kept the letter hidden in my office for days before I felt
emboldened to write:

```
I don't forgive Zvonko, and will not consider
```

writing on his behalf. Our correspondence has
been helpful in allowing me to understand you
and my own reaction to Brian's death, but that
doesn't mean I will ever forgive him.

She wrote back that while she respected my feelings, she was sad that he had to do his time in horrible
prisons compared to the one that she was in, and
that he could see no light at the end. *I don't wish
to manipulate you in any way; that is the last thing I
want . . . You of all people can understand what it means to love
somebody with all your heart.* She said that she had not told
anyone but her parents that she had divorced him, but that she
still loved him and considered him her best friend and confi-
dant.

*Your letters must resurrect a lot of feelings that are
painful to you. I hope you agree that it is still necessary to
work through them. As I read your letters I feel as though
you still want me to suffer. Well, I am still suffering . . .
still in prison 12 years later, and have additionally
experienced many, many hardships while here . . . what
more could I possibly do that I haven't already done to
make amends for my participation? I guess I feel a little
resentful, even though I know emotionally that you have
every right to say what you feel.*

*I am behind walls 24 hours a day. I work mornings in
landscaping and afternoons I am in the computer class. I
came to prison with a university degree, magna cum laude,
and have had to take orders all these years from people
who have never even read a book or had an original idea;
in addition, many of them are unable to handle power,
even though it is illusory power, and abuse it terribly. They
try to strip us of our dignity, to demean us, to treat us like
children or imbeciles or both, but luckily for me, I have
been able to fight this depersonalization. I have remained
my sassy, uncompromising self.*

I read the letter again, and then again, and her words made me feel sullied. I told myself this was the last letter, that I would not write to her again. And for a long time, I kept that promise.

Perhaps it is better to wake up after all, even to suffer,
rather than to remain a dupe to illusions all one's life.
— Kate Chopin, *The Awakening*

Forgiveness

WE CELEBRATED GRACIE'S FIFTIETH BIRTHDAY IN NEW York, and for the first time in recent memory, the whole family came together: my mother in a wheelchair offering a toast to her suntanned daughter, Gracie's son Matthew with his wife and child, and even Corky, who had asked me for the price of a plane ticket from Miami. Gracie and Billy stayed with us that weekend, and after everyone else went to bed, we stayed up late, talking about how wonderful it was to see the family, how it was amazing that we had thrived in the face of our Faile Street beginning, except Corky, who seemed to be unemployed and looked thin and pale despite his Miami address. Although Corky and Gracie lived within driving distance, they didn't communicate. Gracie had grown from those dark days when Corky could still influence her. Now she had a granddaughter, whom she adored. She felt solid, stronger than I had seen her since I was a child.

I missed Gracie terribly when she went home to Florida. I thought of how much my success in life was due to her love and understanding, and thought of the understanding I received from Julie. I realized that it had been almost a year since I stopped writing to Julie and I missed her too, I missed our letters, the excitement, and on a whim, I decided to write to her.

I had written my rage until it began to feel limp and worn like a dress you've put on too many times. And when I started writing her again, I wasn't writing about the rage anymore. I told myself that since she was divorced from Busic, and that he was the real terrorist, I could pick up the correspondence I missed. She seemed the last person left in that Brian stronghold, and I meant to keep Brian alive. When I began to write again, it was to someone who had shared an impossible history that no one else could understand.

I told her about being ostracized from the bomb squad and from Charlie, the friend I thought would support me, and that although it had been over a decade, I still followed his career. When he received a promotion or his name was in the news, I wrote that it should have been Brian's name in that story, Brian wearing those gold bars on his uniform. I wrote to her about the night Charlie came to my door, about the fugue-state I had lived in, and about those first years alone.

For the first time, too, I opened up about how inadequate I felt as a mother. I told her about the time Chris ran away from me in the mall, and when the police found him, he answered *no* when asked if I was his mother. I told her about the time I drove to the hospital twice in one week, once to have Keith's wrist set in a cast, and then Chris's elbow. I told her about Keith's night terrors, times when he woke up screaming for his father and nothing I could say or do would make him feel better.

I wrote about leaving the doctoral program to take care of my premature baby and about how at the time I felt I had lost my direction, the momentum of reading for my orals and meeting with my committee, but that there didn't seem to be time to return to the all-consuming doctoral program. I told her about accepting a job at Suffolk Community College, where I taught writing and literature, a job I had come to love, but mourned the lost opportunity to add PhD to my name.

She was someone I could brag to about my athletic sons, how adorable Kaitlin was. I could complain to her about Keith sneaking a girlfriend into his bedroom, spending Christmas Eve in the hospital with Kaitlin after bronchitis closed her airways, Chris falling off his bike and breaking his clavicle. She had no children, and as long as McTigue kept vigil to keep her in prison, she would stay behind bars and probably never would have them. Yet she wrote of practical ways to handle these everyday challenges. We fell into a rhythm that opened up for me stories of my childhood and of my life with Brian, and in some strange, hidden part of me, it felt right.

I told her about starting what would be a nationwide organization, Survivors of the Shield. Ironic, since I had started SOS because of the devastating blow her actions had on our lives. I did not write how I had been born into poverty, among drug addicts and thieves and had risen to become a woman who could start non-profits and work toward a doctorate degree. I did not say how strange it was that she had been born with everything and had wound up in prison. But the fact of it made me feel strangely smug. It gave me that optimistic buoyant feeling that absolutely anything could happen.

I wondered if that was how forgiveness budded; not with the fanfare of epiphany, but with pain gathering its things, packing up, and slipping away unannounced in the middle of the night.
— Khaled Hosseini, *The Kite Runner*

Saving Julie

GRACIE'S HOUSE ON FILLMORE STREET IN CLEARWATER was white clapboard with blue trim, the porch scattered with wind chimes and geraniums and cane rocking chairs. Inside, the furniture was spare, pale shades of aqua and peach, faded now, the windows shuttered against the bright Florida sun. Rings from glasses stained the coffee table, neglected ashtrays overflowed, and the air smelled of beer and cigarettes.

"Sorry, Kat." Gracie gave me a little smile. "I haven't felt up to housekeeping." Her hair had lost its shine, her ashen face poised on the threshold of whatever malady had taken hold. She waived her hand toward the room, the gesture causing the ash of her cigarette to fall onto the stained rug. The strap of her summer dress slid down her arm where I could see that prison scar, the one everyone thought the result of one of her car accidents.

A profound sadness began to settle in my stomach, and I recalled that in the late 60s, Harry Banks sent Fiona Ryan and me to Ireland to meet with our manufacturers. We extended the trip to include Switzerland and Italy, and Gracie asked if she could come. I made the excuse that it was a work trip, and I couldn't bring her along. But, of course, I could have. Harry would not have cared. That trip changed me, gave me perspective and insight and widened my dreams. Now I wish Gracie had been by my side, her own dreams broadened by the magnificence of the Sistine Chapel, Lake Lucerne, the vivid greens of Ireland. In all her life, Gracie had gotten only as far as Clearwater, a move she envisioned would finally make her happy.

I sat on the sofa next to her. Kaitlin's laughter floated in from the backyard where she was digging for worms with Billy, who promised to take her fishing.

"Don't worry about it. I'm just glad to be here," I said. And I was glad, but the missed opportunities of Gracie's life now seemed like a shield between us. I was the lucky one, the one who went to Europe, married a good guy, graduated college, while a father whose fists were his only means of communication had dashed her dreams.

While we still talked most days, I often felt there was nothing to say, that small talk was a waste of time, that she made her decision to move to a place where she knew no one and where her sole companion was a man who loved his vodka. She didn't want to hear about that from me.

"It's not good," she said. Her lip trembled and her eyes welled up.

Last week she had called to tell me the doctors diagnosed a brain tumor. She pressed the temples of her head. "The reason I've had such bad headaches."

I sat still for a moment, trying to absorb her words. "I'll come down as soon as I can get a flight," I told her. I parceled out my classes, put James in charge of the boys, took Kaitlin out of school, and paid too much for a ticket to Clearwater.

Now I ran my hand over the rough fabric of her sofa. "You'll pull through," I said. And I believed it. Throughout her life, Gracie had been in a head-on collision followed by emergency heart surgery, survived a hit-and-run that shattered her hip, and had been stabbed and survived prison. Gracie, I believed, was invincible.

Her bracelets tinkled together as she took a drag from her cigarette. The silver bangles reminded me of the handcuffs she had once worn, and I thought of Julie's most recent letter, which I had tucked into my purse to read on the plane when only Kaitlin would be watching.

Gracie drummed her fingers against her thigh and looked at me without seeing me. "I don't know this time," she said.

"But didn't you say the doctor could try to remove it?" That burning sensation in my stomach deepened.

Gracie shrugged. "They could try. But I'm not sure I want them to."

I watched as she stared out at the scrubby lawn, and at her skinny husband with yellow teeth and fingertips, who was showing Kaitlin how to dig for bait. The thought hit me slowly: What was here for her? It felt so lonely. Gracie had been through her own hijackings. Addiction had hijacked her dreams, her relationships, her body.

"I'll stay with you," I said quickly. Except staying with Gracie, helping her, meant leaving James alone. Kaitlin was in pre-school, I had the boys to ferry to sports and friends' houses. I needed to teach my classes.

Before Gracie could say yes or no, Kaitlin slammed the screen door, smiling happily, a pail of wiggly slime in her hand. Gracie's eyes were brimming with tears as she lit another cigarette, and then the tears spilled down her cheeks.

While she and Billy set out cold cuts for lunch, I walked around the small rooms with worn beige carpet and looked at memorabilia from Mickey Mantle's in Manhattan and The Lobster Roll in Montauk. In the dining room, my mother's old china cabinet held rows of old photographs in metal frames.

It had been a long time since I'd seen a photo of Brian, and it startled me. Here he was, the man who shaped my life, sitting in a lawn chair in our backyard, beside my mother. She looked happy, a bottle of Budweiser and an ashtray on a small table next to her. Brian was looking at the camera out of shadowy eyes, his usual smile missing. It was one of the pictures that had been in the 1975 album, one of the ones my mother said she had disposed of.

"Where did you get this photo?" I carried the frame into the kitchen and held it out for Gracie to see. It was obvious as her face paled that she had forgotten about it.

"Oh, I found it while we were moving. It was in one of the shoeboxes of photos Mom had tucked away." She tried to recover but the freckles stood out on her cheeks as she realized the gravity of my finding one of the few remaining photos of Brian.

"So, she saved some of Brian's pictures after all," I said, my voice shaking, "even after she knew how angry I was, even after I asked her to move out, even after I told her how much his photos meant to me."

"I'm sorry, Kat," Gracie said as she busied herself with scooping mustard into a little dish. "I thought it was a copy."

"I'd like to have it." I took the back off the frame. "Brian and Mom, 7/17/75," it read in my own handwriting.

ON OUR LAST NIGHT THERE we sat on the porch. Traces of the day's heat lingered while chimes kept rhythm with the breeze. It had turned dark. I could smell the Evening in Paris Gracie always wore, and the tip of her cigarette brightened and faded as she took a drag. The surgery was Wednesday, and Rose had agreed to come down. Rose was a nurse now. I knew it would be better if she were with Gracie on the day of surgery. I was afraid of losing her, afraid of having my heart broken. That night I wasn't sure how to articulate what I felt about my sister, and so we watched the stars come out of a midnight sky and let our silence do the work.

Looking at Gracie's shadowy silhouette I thought about the ways she had influenced my life. She had not only been my sister, she was my champion, the one who took up the slack when my mother had no time, who brushed my hair and read to me, transformed words on the page into stories that only we two shared. When she dreamed of becoming a stewardess I shared her dream, crossed off the days with her. When she returned home after a failed marriage it was I who shared her room, and when she became hooked on drugs it was I who looked for her on deserted city streets. When she went to prison it was me to whom she wrote letters, often enclosing pictures she drew in art class. She told me what it was like to shoot heroin into her veins, the feeling of pure bliss that trumped everything else in the world, knowing I would never try it because of what it did to her. She called me Kat, and I let her even though I hated cats, because Gracie loved me.

ON THE PLANE RIDE HOME, Kaitlin slept across my lap, and I watched the sunset from the air, a fiery orange ball descending, and thought of Julie. I was the only one whose appeal could override McTigue, who kept petitioning to keep the Busics behind bars. Maybe it was time. Maybe since I couldn't help Gracie, I could at least get Julie out of the prison she had made for herself.

When Rose called the following week, I had trouble holding on to the phone. "She wouldn't wake up," Rose said. "I sat with her all afternoon. The doctors said the surgery was successful. I kept asking her to wake up. Then she opened her eyes once."

"Did she say anything?" I asked.

"She just told me, 'no,'" Rose said. "No, she didn't want to wake up. And then she gave up."

Gracie had a kind, loving nature, but she was vulnerable. Her dependence on drugs gave her a cloak of invisibility and made her weak, so that she wasn't able to stand up for herself, and in the end, too weak to live.

It wasn't long after the funeral that I wrote to the parole board to ask for Julie's release. In my grief, the part of me that had somehow always believed I could have saved Gracie thought that I should set a hijacker free.

I took a deep breath and listened
to the old brag of my heart;
I am, I am, I am.
— Sylvia Plath, *The Bell Jar*

Face-to-Face

I received Julie's last letter on a warm October day as the eighties came to a close. In the kitchen, Kaitlin ate the Cheerios I served her for snack while I opened the envelope.

I am so thankful for your letters to me and to the parole board. I will never forget your kindness. I will arrive in New York on the 24th, and I'm so excited to meet you! I know it will be intense, but we have both done enough work on our issues to know how to adequately express our feelings to one another and not get off track.

She sounded so sure of herself.

We would meet at O'Neal's Restaurant across from Central Park. She asked if we might take a walk, and I said yes, but asked that we meet for lunch. I wanted our meeting to be during the daytime, where people would surround us. I felt nervous as the date arrived and had a hard time concentrating. I got out of bed that morning feeling jittery.

"What's the matter?" James wanted to know. I couldn't tell him I was going to do something I knew was dangerous and reckless, but couldn't stop myself. He wouldn't understand. I didn't understand myself.

Looking at my bed I couldn't believe how many dresses I tried on before I ran out of time and finally settled on a black dress with low, comfortable heels. I looked in the mirror at a forty-one-year-old woman. I was still slim, my hair still red, but lines were beginning to appear around my eyes. I wondered if prison life had turned Julie old and gray.

IF I WERE BEING HONEST with myself I would admit that I was afraid of Julie, the woman who slept in the same room with eight sticks of dynamite, who took eighty-six passengers hostage, who fought her way through prison. I was here today on my own. I had lied to my family because there was no way I could convince them a face-to-face with Julie Busic would be in my best interest. It was one thing to write to Julie about how I felt about her, but talking to her in person would take a lot more courage.

As the train passed from the suburban streets of Long Island toward the brilliant skyline of Manhattan, my resolve weakened and my doubts returned. *What if sanctioning her early release was a big mistake? What if she commits another crime? What if she wants revenge for the hateful things I wrote to her?* My foot tapped with a will of its own, my knuckles white around the handle of my handbag. *How can I eat lunch with the terrorist responsible for my husband's death?*

I knew the answer and had known it all along. The connection she had to Brian had somehow brought him into focus for me, and I needed her to keep him alive in my mind.

When the train darkened and roared through the tunnel under the East River I stared at my ghostly reflection and tried to imagine what she looked like. I pictured her many times over the years, reconstructing the image in the photographs from newspapers, but she remained in those photos like a shadow. She wasn't real, and I'll admit I did want to know what she was like, know how someone who grew up in a privileged home could abandon everything for what seemed like a thrill.

I wanted to ask her if spending thirteen years behind bars was worth following the man she ultimately divorced.

I walked along Eighth Avenue intending to catch a bus, but found myself daydreaming about how Julie would look at what I was seeing. I was born in New York and must have walked along Eighth Avenue a hundred times, but today I looked at the streets the way I imagined Julie would see them. They were vibrant, alive with an energy that was invigorating, and before I knew it, I had walked thirty blocks. I stopped in front of Lincoln Center to take in the grandeur of the philharmonic and Alice Tully Hall, feeling pride for my city. The weather was mild, and the walk helped me calm down, and I arrived early and stood outside O'Neal's looking at Central Park, cinnamon leaves scattered along the paths, families of tourists on buggy rides.

And then as I waited at the hostess station someone tapped on my shoulder, and I turned to see Julie Busic. I inhaled sharply. The woman in front of me was stunning, taller than my 5 foot 6 inches, slender, lovely in her blue dress. We were both 41, and I looked for the wear of prison life, but the woman standing there was much prettier than her photos, a natural blue-eyed blonde with even, white teeth. She seemed sophisticated and worldly in a way I feared I would never be.

"Oh my God, you're so beautiful," she said. "I've been waiting for this moment for so long, and here you are."

My insides were shaking. All the words I had practiced were now trapped inside me. I felt the trust I had built through our letters begin to erode. Sounds of the restaurant, traffic beeping, everything was suddenly too loud. I felt faint, and a thin line of perspiration broke out on my lip. I looked down at Julie's shoes, a pair of canvas espadrilles that looked just this minute bought. I wondered if supporters had given her money to buy her outfit, to get her started in her new life. She leaned toward me, and I had the horrible feeling she was about to touch me.

"I'm not sure I should be here," I stammered. All the intimate details I wrote to her seemed sullied now in her presence. "I don't think I can go through with this."

"I understand." Julie tucked her hair behind her ear and talked quickly as though we were in a time jam. "But I came all this way and hope you can give me just a few minutes."

"Table for two?" A bald host in a bowtie beamed at us, and without knowing how, my feet pushed me forward. I followed Julie across the restaurant, smelling a hint of something flowery, Estee Lauder maybe. She was carrying a shopping bag, the kind sold in Hallmark stores. It didn't have a star on it, but for a moment, it frightened me.

The host escorted us to the far side of the room where we were seated at an interior table. The rich, creamy linen napkins were shaped like party hats. Around us, the restaurant bustled with a hundred conversations. At the next table, two women laughed.

"Yesterday I went to a banquet given in my honor," Julie said right away. "It was given by the Croatian community to thank me for my loyalty. They raised money for you and your sons, and gave me a gift for you."

I stared at her. Her supposed loyalty had cost my husband his life, my boys their father. What in hell was I doing here? My eyes turned toward the door.

She saw me and said, "I hope you'll stay. I was so looking forward to meeting you in person," she added.

She handed me the shopping bag. "It's a hand-woven purse from Croatia, and a card with a cash donation." Her voice was soft and cajoling, like her letters, and I felt myself taking the bag. Inside the bag I could see a box wrapped in white paper with bright-colored flowers and red ribbon curling down the sides. It didn't weigh anything. It couldn't be a bomb. I set it next to my chair.

"It must have been hell waiting so long for your freedom." The words tumbled from my mouth, something to say that would inflict some damage, the tone of my voice raw enough to surprise me.

"I thought I would be out in eight years, and I knew I could do that—spend eight years for what I thought was a noble and worthy cause," she said. "We would both be out when we were still in our 30s, and that was doable. We would still have our lives ahead of us. But McTigue held such animosity toward us and did everything he could to keep us locked up far past when we should have been released. He wrote letters and came to our parole hearings—he came all the way to California for mine, and to Pennsylvania for Zvonko's, and told all sorts of lies and distortions about the bombing. He was obsessed with keeping us behind bars."

She looked straight at me and I saw that flash of steel in her eyes. Eight years would have killed me, and yet here she sat only a few weeks free from prison, as defiant as the day she went in.

The two women at the next table toasted to something. They seemed so normal and uncomplicated, and I thought about my life. I had a husband who loved me and children who brought joy into my life. I did not have to be here. I did not have to sit and make conversation with this woman, and again looked toward the door.

"How is your family?" she asked, as though she sensed what I was thinking. "Did you bring photos?"

I did bring photos: James holding Kaitlin in her tiny dance costume. Keith sitting on the front step, Chris in his soccer outfit. But I couldn't show them to this woman who had handed my boys so much confusion, terror, and grief.

"No. I don't have any photos," I lied. In an effort to calm down, I felt myself smoothing my napkin again and again on my lap. I changed the subject. "You're free now. What do you plan to do?"

"I would like to go to Croatia to work with women who were displaced by the war, women who, like Zvonko's mother and sisters, lost everything to the Yugoslavs."

But her letters had said she had planned to live in Oregon, where I had understood she was going to make a new life close to her father the professor, her mother the librarian, and her three well-educated brothers. And now she sat across from me in her new outfit, telling me she was still fighting her ex-husband's cause. She had lied. In another person, I might have admired such steadfast loyalty, but Julie Busic had taken up a place in my life that had drained me. I watched the busboy set down our waters and felt hollowed out.

"Your server will be right with you," the boy said. And in him I saw a flash of Chris, that innocent, green-eyed sweetness that wanted so badly to believe all was right with the world. My boys had learned too early that all was not right, that someone as constant and sure as their father could be torn from them in the glance of a single evening.

"I thought you were divorced," I said as I watched the busboy walk away. "Why would you try to help his family now?"

"Actually," Julie took her napkin from the table and set it on her lap. "We've remarried." She smiled quickly, showing those brilliant white teeth that had not seemed to be bothered by prison. "I've made some hasty decisions, but really, I love my husband, and it's in our best interest to be together."

I looked into her eyes. "Which hasty decision?" I asked. "Hijack a plane? Build a bomb?" My voice rose, and the women at the next table stared openly at us.

"I had no choice," Julie said, leaning forward, her forearms on the table, and I saw the indignation pass over her eyes. "I told you that in my letters. We had to hijack that plane. Zvonko was wanted by the Yugoslav secret police. We were desperate. We thought he would be killed. We had to bring the Croatian situation to the public."

I watched her, and then I saw her again that day she took the witness stand, an indignant young woman who had lied about being pregnant, who had helped hijack a plane and set a bomb in the middle of one of the busiest train stations in the world.

"You had a choice," I said, lowering my voice. "You could have gone to the embassy, the police. You could have paid for your declaration to be printed. You chose to commit a crime. You could have prevented it, Julie."

And then our waiter was beside us, a pad in his hand. "Do

you ladies need a few more minutes?" he asked.

"Yes," I told him. "Please."

"Look," Julie said when he had gone. "There has to be an end to our suffering. You said yourself that we paid our debt to society. Which brings me to ask again if you would consider writing a letter on Zvonko's behalf?" She ran her finger around the rim of her water glass and smiled, as though she were sharing a friendly lunch with a girlfriend. "I really hate to ask, but I know you would do the same if you were in my position."

Around us people clinked glasses, ate shrimp scampi and drank chardonnay, and in the middle of this seemingly normal day, I saw that I had not only used Julie Busic, she had used me. Her real motivation all along had been to save herself and Zvonko Busic. All the cajoling and confiding had been artifice.

Out of the yellow paper and the pens they gave her in prison, she had made for herself a stage, whereby she could play at regret and apology and seduce me with her life story. She could play at being fascinated by me, so that one day I would set her free. I had hidden her letters from my husband, had lowered my guard and allowed us to become friends. I had let a criminal into my life.

As she sat there smiling at me expectantly, I understood that all this time she had been trying to save herself and her husband. And I had been trying to save myself from the pain of being a widow, pain of the boys losing their father, pain of not being heard when I asked why that bomb exploded, pain of losing my lawsuit to the City of New York, pain of not growing up with the opportunities Julie had: the white picket fence and the middle-class income. It was always easy, when Gracie and I were sharing books across the bedroom we shared, to believe in the fictional worlds those pages spun for us. And I knew now, with Julie sitting in front of me, that Julie's letters had been just that, a fairytale I had wanted to believe.

I closed my menu and set it aside. I wasn't that little girl from the Bronx anymore. I wasn't begging for dollars from my father in front of Horn & Hardart, or getting punched by a brother after he stole my camera. I wasn't crying because I thought my mother didn't care about me or because Gracie was lost to the streets. I was Kathleen Murray Moran, wife, mother, educator. I no longer needed saving, least of all from this woman who wasn't any kind of savior. She was just a hijacker, dressed in very pretty clothing.

I set my napkin on the table. "I'm not going to help him get out of jail," I told her. "As a matter of fact, I'm going do everything in my power to keep him locked up for the rest of his life." I scraped back the chair. "I'm leaving." I stood up.

"Wait, please."

But I didn't wait. The Busics had hijacked me before when I was a young mother with two boys, and I let myself be hijacked a second time when I thought she might take away the pain. But it had taken meeting the hijacker face-to-face to understand that I was tired of being hijacked. I was ready to be free. I turned and walked across the room, leaving Julie Busic and the gift she brought from her supporters sitting beside the chair.

Life's but a walking shadow, a poor player
That struts and frets his hour upon the stage
And then is heard no more.
— William Shakespeare, *Macbeth*

Full Circle

The words I wrote to Julie to unburden my soul seemed tainted now, but strangely enough, I did not regret getting to know Julie Busic. I did not wish I had never written to her, as those letters allowed me to grow in ways I had not realized. I thought about how ironic life was as I rode the elevator up to Governor Mario Cuomo's office. The bill that Susan, Mary Beth, and I had been working so hard for over the last few years was finally going to be signed in the presence of senators and countless media.

From the fifty-eighth floor, jackhammers and car horns in the financial district below were silenced, and through the wall of glass windows a tugboat streamed along the Hudson toward the Statue of Liberty, rising above the river like a phoenix. It was a New York day, filtered sunshine with smokestacks filling the air with promise. We'd met with the Governor once before on a freezing cold day in February when the sky was a brilliant blue and the waves held white caps. Sitting across from him then, we had given him our wish list, the things that would improve our lives and those of our children: the right to remarry without losing our pensions, scholarships for ourselves and our offspring, grief counseling training so we could console new widows. He added two monuments for fallen police and fire officers, one in Battery Park City, and one in Albany, and special license plates with the Survivors of the Shield logo.

A glint of sun caught the governor's eyeglasses that winter day as he put down the pen he used to make notes. "Let me talk to my senators," he said. "Garner support in Albany."

Celebrating with a glass of wine afterward, Susan told us, "Sometimes dreams do come true." But the year following had been hard, trips to Albany were canceled because senators weren't available, there had been delays over appropriating funds, and sometimes it looked like it was never going to happen. Except now we were standing in his office. It was springtime, the view greener, and the conference room smelled of rich coffee and baked goods. I watched the wind catch the sail of a cutter as it headed up the East River.

"Hey Murray." The governor came up beside me. "What do you do when you're not pushing for legislation?"

"English professor," I said, enjoying the look on his face that said I'd made an impression. His heavy dark eyebrows rose toward his brow. "Shakespeare?"

"I'm teaching *Macbeth* this semester." I couldn't hold back my smile as his widened.

"I count myself a Shakespeare aficionado," he said. He squinted his eyes and thought for a moment. "How about a Shakespeare challenge?" The cutter blew along the whitecaps, its sails majestic against the Brooklyn skyline. I stepped back from the window to face him.

"I accept your challenge, Governor."

Excellent," he said. "The subject is *Macbeth*. Over lunch we will ask three questions each. The winner gets a Montblanc pen, courtesy of this office," and just as I was saying, "You're on," the press arrived, a flurry of cameras and microphones. The office's press secretary rounded us up to stand behind the governor's desk, New York's top notable figures and three police widows.

"Governor Cuomo wants to have a literary contest with me," I whispered to Mary Beth while the flashbulbs went off. I felt a surge of joy. I could never have conjured up this scene in a million years. Kathy Martin, the kid who slept on the top bunk in the basement apartment on Faile Street, was now standing next to the governor of the State of New York, and through my tenacity and diligence, the lives of every New York police and fire widow would change. No one else would have to fake a marriage or lie about it. My sons and the hundreds of sons and daughters who lost their father, children who had not considered higher education, would now go to college. As an educator, I was elated. As a South Bronx kid, I stood tall and let myself be counted.

All the major networks filmed as Governor Mario Cuomo signed the COPS Agenda, changing the path of those unfortunate enough to lose their spouses in the line of duty.

"The bill includes every New York State police and fire department," the governor told the press, "including scholarships for survivors of volunteer fireman, and it has all come about as a result of the hard work of Kathleen Murray, Susan McCormack, and Mary Beth O'Neill."

Afterward, we sat across from each other in the dining room, the governor and I, our plates piled high with sandwiches and salads. While we were standing around his desk I thought about the questions I composed for my *Macbeth* final, the ones we went over in class that were the first to be answered, a tactic I used to ease students into the more comprehensive questions that would come later. I would start with those now as well.

I taught *Macbeth* for the first time when I was a doctoral student. Then I stood before a podium in an auditorium with sixty or so students, all eyes on me, waiting to be enlightened on the Bard. I lectured from notes, unsure of myself. Now, over a decade later, having read the play scores of times, I no longer lectured. Instead, I gathered students into groups where they hashed out the language and the hidden interpretations and enlightened the class on their newfound appreciation of the master.

"Okay, Murray," Governor Cuomo said, when we were settled. "First question: What did Lady Macbeth say when she thinks she sees blood on her hands?"

I smiled. He, too, would start with easy ones. "Out damned spot," I answered.

We were a table of eight, including Matilda Cuomo, the first lady who had come to lend her support to police widows, Mary Beth, Susan, Jimmy Lysaght, Senator Dean Skelos, and the chief of police. Everyone at the table turned to listen as the Governor announced, "Correct! One for you."

It was great fun for me, my territory, and I felt at ease and confident.

I asked, "What do the weird sisters predict?" He couldn't help but grin at the anticipated question and waited a second.

Waving his fork in the air like a conductor, he said, "That Macbeth would become thane of Cawdor."

"Yes, Governor, you are correct. We're tied."

"Now, tell me," he asked as he dug into his plate of pasta salad. "How does Lady Macbeth comfort Macbeth when he begins to hallucinate?"

I waited a few seconds like I was considering the answer, but I knew it. The question was Shakespeare 101. "She comforts him by putting him to bed," I answered.

"Your second question is," I waited for the imaginary drum-roll, "what makes Duncan a good king?" It was an open question, the answers often varied, and I gave credit to anyone who suggested that Duncan was a people's king.

He knew the answer right off, I could tell. "Duncan is kind and generous." I felt the excitement rise up a notch. *I could lose this,* I thought. *I will need to dig deeper into my bag of* Macbeth *trivia.*

"Again, you are correct," I said. "We are tied at two each. Give me your best shot, Governor, or go home empty-handed."

"You got it." He mimed a serious face before he asked his last question, "Why is Macduff able to kill Macbeth despite the witches' prophecy?"

It was a really good question, one that had to do with Macbeth's statement after he slays young Siward and announces that no man who is of woman born is a threat to Macbeth, but it was a question any learned Shakespearean would know. "Macduff was born by cesarean section," I said, and waited for his reaction.

"Yes!" he declared. He was laughing now, animated, his eyes bright. There were smiles around the table, everyone waiting to see who would falter. I leaned forward and asked my last question, one I used to challenge my students. "Why is it Banquo and not King Duncan who haunts Macbeth?"

The governor squeezed his bushy eyebrows together as he thought over the question. He looked at his wife with a knowing smile before answering. "Because Macbeth is more troubled over murdering a king than a thane." I popped a grape in my mouth and waited to see if he was going to revise his answer before I gave the correct one, as I would have done if I were in front of my class.

When he beamed at me as though the contest was a draw, I said, no, not quite. "Banquo was a greater threat because he heard the witches' prophesy and knew of Macbeth's ambition to become king." He looked surprised and then realized his error.

"That's right. I should have known that." His smile lit up his face and everyone at the table clapped, and the governor took from his pocket a box containing a black pen with the white star on top.

We celebrated that afternoon, Mary Beth and Susan and I, and reveled in our accomplishment. It had been fourteen years since Brian died, and during most of that time I felt subjugated, at the mercy of the powers that be. Now I knew I had a voice and my voice was heard.

For a long time after I left Julie sitting at the table in O'Neal's, I would feel the sting of shame when I thought about her, that I had believed in her as an ally, that I had been seduced by her in the same way cult members talk about a kind of brainwashing that happens in the darkest, weakest corners of their mind. I don't know if Terry McTigue ever knew that I was instrumental in Julie's release, but it didn't matter anymore.

As I moved about my life and realized what I had accomplished, I found that Julie became just an ordinary woman who had committed an egregious crime, believing it would make her extraordinary, and the aura I had built around her crumbled and remodeled into someone as indistinctive as a passerby.

What could, what should be done with all the time
now before us, open and unshaped, feather-light in its
freedom and lead-heavy in its uncertainty?
— Pascal Mercier, *Night Train to Lisbon*

Aftermath

1990

On a warm summer day, James waited at the altar and I walked down the church aisle. As I stood before the priest, James took my hand and, finally, we were pronounced husband and wife. It had taken time, but James did forgive me for deceiving him. He said he didn't understand why I didn't trust him to support me, and I realized that he was right. James was a man who would always love and support me.

That fall I drove Keith two and a half hours to SUNY New Paltz. The roads were wet and clouds laced the sky. Keith sat up front with me, Kaitlin buckled in her car seat behind. I thought about how my eldest son had gotten to this day: night terrors as a child, his shaved head and black outfits as a teenager. Last summer he followed the Grateful Dead and had not called for a week. He had not wanted Fordham in the Bronx where I could visit regularly. He was ready to be on his own.

The ride was mostly quiet as we watched the landscape pass. And then when we hit the thruway he said, "You know what, mom?"

"What?" I glanced over and noticed the shadow of a beard

and saw again the day he sat on the bathroom sink while Brian shaved, his little face covered with foam as he watched his father. Today he looked a lot like his father, auburn hair cut short, square jaw, blue eyes.

"I was thinking about Brian. I know he was a hero. But I only knew him as perfect, never as a father or a man." I watched him follow a raindrop down the windowpane with his finger. "But I think the real hero in my life is you." He looked over at me. "You raised me, you taught me right from wrong, you changed laws." He grinned. "I hope I can do half as much stuff as you did."

Tears laced my eyelashes. My heart swelled with pride. He had never said words like that before. "Oh Keith, that's so sweet. Thank you."

We passed the rest of the time in quiet contentment and watched the sun come out, and as we drove onto campus Kaitlin read the sign.

"Sunny New Paltz," she called out. We laughed. Sun glinted off the windows of the campus buildings.

"Well, here we are," Keith said.

"Yes," I told him. "We finally arrived."

Epilogue

It was drizzling when the bomb squad van pulled up to Penn Station to pick us up for the trip to the West Village, a joy ride for my grandchildren with lights and sirens to part traffic. We were the guests of honor, there to co-name Charles Street *Police Officer Brian Murray Way* to honor a member of the bomb squad killed in the line of duty on September 11, 1976. Now it was 2014, and they had put up barricades to block traffic. A tent sheltered commissioners and chiefs and uniform police from the rain. Bomb trucks lined the curb, doors open, exposing robots and remote-control devices and every kind of protective gear available.

I never expected this kind of affirmation and recognition of our sacrifice. I thought a few of the members from the old bomb squad would gather for the unveiling, and watched in vain for Charlie, but even his absence and the rain couldn't dampen the day. Today was a celebration. My sons, successful businessmen, mingled with dignitaries, and my grandchildren played in the street with a bomb-seeking robot. A gentleman I had never met offered his hand.

"I was a patrolman with Brian," he told me, "and was deeply affected by his death. As a result, I decided to go into law instead of law enforcement. Now I am a judge."

I felt a swell of pride, not grief, over the loss of a good man, and gratification at how many lives he touched. Keith stood before the microphone and spoke to the crowd of men who knew his father as he never had.

"We need only one light to guide us home," he said, "and I was fortunate enough to have two, Brian Murray, whose light shone from heaven, and James Moran who walked by my side and showed me the way."

Dignitaries on a dais spoke of heroism and bravery, how the bomb squad back then had dismantled devices in civilian clothes. A street re-naming is reserved for men like Brian Murray who saved lives, they said, trained to go where the rest of the NYPD cannot.

Spectators gathered at the corner, even when the rain began in earnest, and watched my grandchildren remove the shroud covering the new name of the street. It was a day I felt appreciation for the grand gesture by the City of New York and the New York Police Department, who in the end never forgot their own.

I missed Gracie. I always did on days like this. I wanted her to see the boys all grown up, fathers themselves now. And I missed my mother, who died in that nursing home surrounded by her family. My father died alone in his Brooklyn apartment, Corky followed a few years later.

Zvonko Busic was finally released from prison after thirty-two years. And as she told me on that October afternoon almost twenty years before, Julie went to Croatia to wait for him. Once there, she was put on a no-fly list and refused reentry into the U.S. When Zvonko returned to his home country, he was given a hero's parade. But a few years later, after failing to assimilate into society, he left a suicide note and put a bullet in his head.

Sometimes, driving to teach an early morning class at Suffolk Community College, I think about those mornings I used to wake up in the basement apartment on Faile Street where I took my usual spot on the edge of the claw foot tub. There I watched my mother put on her makeup, cover the bruises my father left, and, as she rolled up her silk stockings with the seam up the back, asked, "Are they on straight?"

Perhaps we're in jeopardy of being hijacked more often than we think. For my mother, the hijacker was a father who married her off at sixteen to an alcoholic she didn't love, Gracie's hijacker was her addiction, Brian's was an obsessed political fanatic and his wife. But for those children and fathers and sisters and widows who are left behind, perhaps we have a choice, to be hijacked again, or to make the sometimes difficult, often-complex choice for freedom, instead.

Brian and Kathleen Murray
Police Academy Graduation, May, 1970

Brian Murray (l) and Charlie Wells (r)
Bomb Squad Section, 1975

Gracie with Matthew, 1961

Chris Murray, Age 2, 1976

Keith Murray, Age 4, 1976

Department of Transportation Medal Ceremony
Kathleen with Terence McTigue (r), 1977

James and Kathleen Moran, 1979

Brian Murray, 1976

Funeral of Brian Murray
Kathleen with Bobby Tellone (l) and Paul Eckelmann (r)
September, 1976

Julie Busic with passenger of hijacked Flight 533, 1976

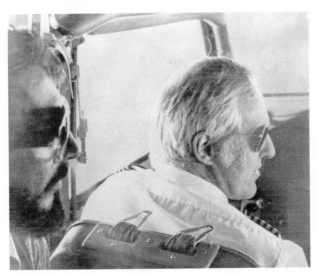

Zvonko Busic (l) in cockpit with Captain Carey during hijacking
September 10, 1976

Kathleen with New York State Governor Mario Cuomo, 1979

Survivors of the Shield Bill Signing
Back row: New York State Senators
Front row: (l-r) Kathleen Murray, Susan McCormack,
Governor Mario Cuomo, Mary Beth O'Neill

Street Renaming of Police Officer Brian Murray Way
October, 2014

Acknowledgements

Suzanne Kingsbury, my directional editor, mentor, shoulder to cry on, and everlasting friend, your brilliant ideas helped shape my story, for which you have my heartfelt thanks.

To my agents, Laura Rothschild, whose enthusiasm brought this book into the light, and Sandra O'Donnell, who saw what I didn't and polished every word.

To my brothers and sisters, to whom I am grateful for giving my life such richness and diversity. Thank you to my mother, long deceased, but never out of my thoughts, and to Gracie, who loved me when no one else did.

Huge gratitude to my writing buddies, Rochelle Donnino, who lived this dream with me, Dede Cummings, who began our voyage together, Charlotte DeKanter Chung, Amanda Skelton, Sharisse Smith, Kyle Minor, Kate Goehring, and Lynne Kramer, who helped steer me toward my goal. Special thanks to Tony Curto, for his sound advice.

To Dayna Anderson, Kayla Church, Cami Wasden, and the staff at Amberjack, thank you for the amazing opportunity.

Most of all, thank you to my husband James, who stood aside while I wrote about a life that came before, and encouraged me always to just write. And to my children, Keith, who cheered me on, Chris, who believed I could do it, his wife Dayna, my number one cheerleader, Kaitlin, who listened to my endless stories and offered sound feedback, and her husband, Grant Lacey, who praised my efforts at every turn. And to my grandchildren, Olivia, Finnegan, and Lillian, who are proud their Mema wrote a book.

About the Author

Kathleen Murray Moran holds a BA in Journalism (Magna cum Laude) and an MA in English from SUNY Stony Brook. She has taught writing and literature at Suffolk Community College for twenty-five years.

She is the widow of Brian Murray, and the co-founder of Survivors of the Shield (SOS). As a cofounder of SOS, a New York City police widows' organization providing social, economic, and emotional support to surviving spouses of police killed in the line of duty, Kathleen has given speeches in front of audiences of over one thousand people, has helped organize and secure funding for the bomb squad's 100th anniversary dinner, has appeared on Sixty Minutes, NBC Live at Five, and given numerous interviews.

She was also instrumental in passing legislation that led to former Governor Mario Cuomo's COPS Agenda. She has worked with State Senator Dean Skelos to establish full scholarships for line of duty widows and children to all SUNY schools, and a four-year scholarship to St. John's University. She has worked with the office of the governor of New York, Crime Victims Board, and the Commissioner of Motor Vehicles, to ensure officers killed in the line of duty are recognized and to secure benefits for their families.

Kathleen has met with Mayors Dinkins, Koch, Giuliani and Bloomberg, Commissioner Ray Kelly, and PBA President, Patrick Lynch, to ensure the continuing cooperation between the City of New York and police widows. She met with Mayor Giuliani to ensure the continued incarceration of Zvonko Busic, the Croatian terrorist who spearheaded the hijacking of TWA flight 335 on September 11, 1976. She worked with Mayor DeBlasio and Councilwoman Christine Quinn's office to rename the Charles Street corner of Bleecker Street in New York City, Police Officer Brian Murray Way, which was dedicated in an official ceremony on October 1, 2014.

In 2014, an excerpt from her memoir went viral on Salon. com (it was listed as the #3 Life story of the year). Another excerpt was shortlisted for the Huff Post/AARP memoir award and guest judge Rita Wilson called her story, "one of the very best pieces our judges encountered." A podcast was recorded for NPR's Snap Judgment (the segment earned Atlantic Monthly's Top-Fifty spot). Her story has been showcased on NPR Ireland, Vancouver Public Radio, and Comcast X/Finity. Kathleen has recently been approached by 20/20 to participate in a feature on forgiveness.

She lives on Long Island where she organizes writing and book groups. Kathleen is currently working on her first novel.